JOHN
MACARTHUR

1&2 TIMOTHY

Encouragement for Church Leaders

THOMAS NELSON
Since 1798

NASHVILLE   DALLAS   MEXICO CITY   RIO DE JANEIRO   BEIJING

1 & 2 TIMOTHY
MACARTHUR BIBLE STUDIES

Copyright © 2007 John F. MacArthur, Jr.

Published in Nashville, Tennessee. Thomas Nelson is a trademark of Thomas Nelson, Inc.

Thomas Nelson, Inc. titles may be purchased in bulk for education, business, fundraising, or sales promotional use. For information, please email SpecialMarkets@ThomasNelson.com.

Published in association with the literary agency of Wolgemuth & Associates, Inc.

Produced with the assistance of the Livingstone Corporation. Project staff include Jake Barton, Betsy Todt Schmitt, and Andy Culbertson.

Project editors: Mary Horner Collins, Amber Rae, and Len Woods.

Scripture quotations marked NKJV are taken from the The New King James Version®. Copyright © 1982 by Thomas Nelson, Inc. Used by permission. All rights reserved.

"Keys to the Text" material taken from the following sources:

1 Corinthians. MacArthur New Testament Commentary Series. Copyright © 1984, 1996 by John MacArthur. Published by Moody Press, Chicago, Illinois. Used by permission.

The MacArthur Study Bible (electronic ed.). John MacArthur, General Editor. Copyright © 1997 by Word Publishing. All rights reserved. Used by permission.

Nelson's New Illustrated Bible Dictionary, Rev. ed. R. F. Youngblood, F. F. Bruce, R. K. Harrison, editors. Copyright © 1995 by Thomas Nelson Publishers. Used by permission.

Our Sufficiency in Christ (electronic ed.) Copyright © 1997 by John F. MacArthur. Published by Word Publishing: Dallas, Texas. Use by permission.

Cover Art by Kirk Luttrell, Livingstone Corporation
Interior Design and Composition by Joel Bartlett, Livingstone Corporation

ISBN-10: 1-4185-0887-X
ISBN-13: 978-141850-887-6

Printed in the United States of America.
07 08 09 10 RRD 9 8 7 6 5 4 3 2 1

CONTENTS

Introduction to 1 Timothy

This is the first of two inspired letters Paul wrote to his beloved son in the faith. Timothy received his name, which means "one who honors God," from his mother (Eunice) and grandmother (Lois), devout Jews who became believers in the Lord Jesus Christ (2 Tim. 1:5). They taught Timothy the Old Testament Scriptures from his childhood (2 Tim. 3:15). His father was a Greek (Acts 16:1) who may have died before Timothy met Paul.

Timothy was from Lystra (Acts 16:1–3), a city in the Roman province of Galatia (part of modern Turkey). Paul led Timothy to Christ (1:2, 18; 1 Cor. 4:17; 2 Tim. 1:2), undoubtedly during his ministry in Lystra on his first missionary journey (Acts 14:6–23). When he revisited Lystra on his second missionary journey, Paul chose Timothy to accompany him (Acts 16:1–3). Although Timothy was very young (probably in his late teens or early twenties, since about fifteen years later Paul referred to him as a young man, 4:12), he had a reputation for godliness (Acts 16:2). Timothy was to be Paul's disciple, friend, and co-laborer for the rest of the apostle's life, ministering with him in Berea (Acts 17:14), Athens (Acts 17:15), and Corinth (Acts 18:5; 2 Cor. 1:19), and accompanying him on his trip to Jerusalem (Acts 20:4). He was with Paul in his first Roman imprisonment and went to Philippi (2:19–23) after Paul's release. In addition, Paul frequently mentions Timothy in his epistles (Rom. 16:21; 2 Cor. 1:1; Phil. 1:1; Col. 1:1; 1 Thess. 1:1; 2 Thess. 1:1; Philem. 1). Paul often sent Timothy to churches as his representative (1 Cor. 4:17; 16:10; Phil. 2:19; 1 Thess. 3:2), and 1 Timothy finds him on another assignment, serving as pastor of the church at Ephesus (1:3). According to Hebrews 13:23, Timothy was imprisoned somewhere and released.

Author and Date

Many modernist critics delight in attacking the plain statements of Scripture and, for no good reason, deny that Paul wrote the Pastoral Epistles (1, 2 Tim., Titus). Ignoring the testimony of the letters themselves (1:1; 2 Tim. 1:1; Titus 1:1) and that of the early church (which is as strong for the Pastoral Epistles as for any of Paul's epistles, except Romans and 1 Corinthians), these critics maintain that a devout follower of Paul wrote the Pastoral Epistles in the second century. As proof, they offer five lines of supposed evidence: (1) the historical references in the Pastoral Epistles cannot be harmonized with the chronology of Paul's life given in Acts;

(2) the false teaching described in the Pastoral Epistles is the fully developed Gnosticism of the second century; (3) the church organizational structure in the Pastoral Epistles is that of the second century and is too well developed for Paul's day; (4) the Pastoral Epistles do not contain the great themes of Paul's theology; and (5) the Greek vocabulary of the Pastoral Epistles contains many words not found in Paul's other letters, nor in the rest of the New Testament.

While it is unnecessary to dignify such unwarranted attacks by unbelievers with an answer, occasionally such an answer does enlighten. Thus, in reply to the critics' arguments, the following points are given: (1) This contention of historical incompatibility is valid only if Paul was never released from his Roman imprisonment mentioned in Acts. But he was released, since Acts does not record Paul's execution, and Paul himself expected to be released (Phil. 1:19, 25–26; 2:24; Philem. 22). The historical events in the Pastoral Epistles do not fit into the chronology of Acts because they happened after the close of the Acts narrative, which ends with Paul's first imprisonment in Rome. (2) While there are similarities between the heresy of the Pastoral Epistles and second-century Gnosticism, there are also important differences. Unlike second-century Gnosticism, the false teachers of the Pastoral Epistles were still within the church (see 1:3–7), and their teaching was based on Judaistic legalism (1:7; Titus 1:10, 14; 3:9). (3) The church organizational structure mentioned in the Pastoral Epistles is, in fact, consistent with that established by Paul (Acts 14:23; Phil. 1:1). (4) The Pastoral Epistles do mention the central themes of Paul's theology, including the inspiration of Scripture (2 Tim. 3:15–17); election (2 Tim. 1:9; Titus 1:1–2); salvation (Titus 3:5–7); the deity of Christ (Titus 2:13); His mediatory work (1 Tim. 2:5); and substitutionary atonement (2:6). (5) The different subject matter in the Pastoral Epistles required a different vocabulary from that in Paul's other epistles. Certainly a pastor today would use a different vocabulary in a personal letter to a fellow pastor than he would in a work of systematic theology.

The idea that a "pious forger" wrote the Pastoral Epistles faces several further difficulties: (1) The early church did not approve of such practices and surely would have exposed this as a ruse, if there had actually been one (see 2 Thess. 2:1–2; 3:17). (2) Why forge three letters that include similar material and no deviant doctrine? (3) If a counterfeit, why not invent an itinerary for Paul that would have harmonized with Acts? (4) Would a later, devoted follower of Paul have put the words of 1 Timothy 1:13, 15 into his master's mouth? (5) Why would he include warnings against deceivers (2 Tim. 3:13; Titus 1:10), if he himself were one?

The evidence seems clear that Paul wrote 1 Timothy and Titus shortly after his release from his first Roman imprisonment (about AD 62–64), and then wrote 2 Timothy from prison during his second Roman imprisonment (about AD 66–67), shortly before his death.

BACKGROUND AND SETTING

After being released from his first Roman imprisonment (see Acts 28:30), Paul revisited several of the cities in which he had ministered, including Ephesus. Leaving Timothy behind there to deal with problems that had arisen in the Ephesian church, such as false doctrine (1:3–7; 4:1–3; 6:3–5), disorder in worship (2:1–15), the need for qualified leaders (3:1–14), and materialism (6:6–19), Paul went on to Macedonia, from where he wrote Timothy this letter to help him carry out his task in the church (see 3:14–15).

HISTORICAL AND THEOLOGICAL THEMES

First Timothy is a practical letter containing pastoral instruction from Paul to Timothy (see 3:14–15). Since Timothy was well versed in Paul's theology, the apostle had no need to give him extensive doctrinal instruction. This epistle does, however, express many important theological truths, such as the proper function of the law (1:5–11), salvation (1:14–16; 2:4–6); the attributes of God (1:17); the Fall (2:13–14); the person of Christ (3:16; 6:15–16); election (6:12); and the second coming of Christ (6:14–15).

INTERPRETIVE CHALLENGES

Scholars disagree over the identity of the false teachers (1:3) and the genealogies (1:4) involved in their teaching. What it means to be "delivered to Satan" (1:20) has also been a source of debate. The letter contains key passages in the debate over the extent of the atonement (2:4–6; 4:10). Paul's teaching on the role of women (2:9–15) has generated much discussion, particularly his declaration that they are not to assume leadership roles in the church (2:11–12). How women can be saved by bearing children (2:15) has also confused many. Whether the fact that an elder must be "the husband of one wife" excludes divorced or unmarried men has been disputed, as well as whether Paul refers to deacons' wives or deaconesses (3:11). Those who believe Christians can lose their salvation cite 4:1 as support for their view. There is a question about the identity of the widows in 5:3–16—are they needy women ministered to by the church, or an order of older women ministering to the church? Does "double honor" accorded to elders who rule well (5:17–18) refer to respect or money? These will all be dealt with in the notes provided by the passages.

NOTES

_____

_____

_____

_____

_____

_____

_____

_____

_____

_____

_____

_____

_____

_____

_____

_____

_____

_____

_____

_____

_____

_____

_____

_____

_____

_____

_____

~ I ~
BEWARE OF FALSE DOCTRINE!

1 Timothy 1:1–20

DRAWING NEAR

Paul had a miraculous encounter with Christ that turned his life around. He calls himself an "insolent man" who had received God's mercy and grace. What person do you know (or have heard about) who has an amazing "before-and-after" testimony of how God transformed his or her life? What about that person's story encourages you?

_____

_____

_____

Why is it important to know what you believe, and why you believe it?

_____

_____

_____

As you begin this study, ask God to show you more about His mercy and grace.

_____

_____

_____

THE CONTEXT

In two brief verses that introduce the letter, the apostle Paul demonstrates his great concern for the church at Ephesus. His passion was the result of three years of ministry there. In order to help his young protégé battle the false teaching that was infiltrating the church, Paul threw all of his apostolic authority behind the young pastor. Not only that, Paul also prayed that God would give his beloved child in the faith the grace, mercy, and peace needed to navigate a difficult situation.

Despite its rich spiritual history, the Ephesian church was targeted by false teachers just as Paul had warned (Acts 20:29–30). Paul wrote this epistle to prepare Timothy for the onslaught of these enemies of the gospel. The opening charge in 1:3–11 sets the stage for all that will follow. Paul discusses four things that are true of false teachers: their doctrinal deviations, their mission, their motives, and their legacy.

Some scholars argue that Paul's words in verses 12 through 17 are a parenthetical thought unrelated to the flow of thought in 1 Timothy. This is a weak argument, however, in light of Paul's overall purpose. Paul's intent was to warn his young associate of the dangers of the false teachers. Since they were teaching an erroneous view of the law, Paul purposed to show how a proper understanding of the law results in conviction of sin and an appreciation of grace. Here then is a contrast between the glory of the true gospel and the bankruptcy of false doctrine.

Keys to the Text

Ephesus: Timothy was in the city of Ephesus, the capital of the Roman province of Asia (Asia Minor, modern Turkey). Located at the mouth of the Cayster River, on the east side of the Aegean Sea, Ephesus was perhaps best known for its magnificent temple of Artemis, or Diana, one of the seven wonders of the ancient world. It was also an important political, educational, and commercial center, ranking with Alexandria in Egypt and Antioch of Pisidia, in southern Asia Minor. The church here may have been started by Priscilla and Aquila, a gifted couple, who had been left in Ephesus by Paul on his second missionary journey (Acts 18:18–19). Later, Paul firmly established this fledgling church on his third missionary journey (Acts 19), and he pastored it for some three years. After Paul left, Timothy pastored the congregation for perhaps a year and a half.

The Law: The Mosaic law is in view here, not just law in general. Paul said that the would-be teachers wanted to impose circumcision and the keeping of Mosaic ceremonies on the church as necessary for salvation. These "Judaizers" plagued the early church, attempting to add to the gospel the legalistic requirements of the Old Testament. The law is good or useful because it reflects God's holy will and righteous standard (Ps. 19:7; Rom. 7:12) and accomplishes its purpose in showing sinners their sin and their need for a Savior (Rom. 3:19; Gal. 3:24).

Unleashing the Text

Read 1:1–20, noting the key words and definitions next to the passage.

1 Timothy 1:1–20 (NKJV)

1 *Paul, an apostle of Jesus Christ, by the commandment of God our Savior and the Lord Jesus Christ, our hope,*

2 *To Timothy, a true son in the faith: Grace, mercy, and peace from God our Father and Jesus Christ our Lord.*

3 *As I urged you when I went into Macedonia— remain in Ephesus that you may charge some that they teach no other doctrine,*

4 *nor give heed to fables and endless genealogies, which cause disputes rather than godly edification which is in faith.*

apostle of Jesus Christ (v. 1)— "One who is sent with a commission." An apostle was chosen and trained by Jesus Christ to proclaim His truth during the formative years of the church. Because Paul was not among the original Twelve, he needed to defend his apostleship (see 2 Cor. 12:11–12; Acts 1:2; 2:42; Eph. 2:20).

God our Savior (v. 1)—This is a title unique to the Pastoral Epistles (1 & 2 Tim., Titus) that has its roots in the Old Testament (Ps. 25:5; 27:9; Mic. 7:7; Hab. 3:18). God is by nature a saving God and the source of our salvation.

Jesus Christ, our hope (v. 1)—Christians have hope for the future because Christ purchased salvation for them on the cross in the past (Rom. 5:1–2), sanctifies them through His Spirit in the present (Gal. 5:16–25), and will lead them to glory in the future.

true son in the faith (v. 2)—Only Timothy and Titus received this special expression of Paul's favor. The Greek word for "son" is better translated "child," which emphasizes Paul's role as spiritual father to Timothy. "True" speaks of the genuineness of Timothy's faith (see 2 Tim. 1:5). Timothy was Paul's most cherished pupil and protégé (1 Cor. 4:17).

Grace, mercy, and peace (v. 2)—This familiar greeting of Paul's appears in all his epistles (see Rom. 1:7), but with the addition here of "mercy" (see 2 Tim. 1:2). Mercy frees believers from the misery that accompanies the consequences of sin.

when I went into Macedonia—remain in Ephesus (v. 3)—Before Paul left Ephesus, he likely began the confrontation with the expulsion of Hymenaeus and Alexander (v. 20), then assigned Timothy to stay on and complete what he had begun.

charge (v. 3)—This refers to a military command; it demands that a subordinate obey an order from a superior (see 2 Tim. 4:1).

some (v. 3)—The false teachers were few in number yet had a wide influence. Several reasons point toward these men being elders in the church at Ephesus and in the churches in the surrounding region: (1) they presumed to be teachers (v. 7), a role reserved for elders (3:2; 5:17); (2) Paul himself had to excommunicate Hymenaeus and Alexander, which implies they occupied the highest pastoral positions; (3) Paul detailed the qualifications of an elder (3:1–7), implying that unqualified men, who needed to be replaced by qualified ones, were occupying those roles; (4) Paul stressed that sinning elders were to be publicly disciplined (5:19–22).

teach no other doctrine (v. 3)—This is a compound word made up of two Greek words that mean "of a different kind" and "to teach." The false teachers were teaching doctrine different from apostolic doctrine (see 6:3–4; Gal. 1:6–7); this had to do with the gospel of salvation. Apparently they were teaching another gospel and not the "glorious gospel of the blessed God" (v. 11).

fables and endless genealogies (v. 4)—Legends and fanciful stories manufactured from elements of Judaism (v. 7; see Titus 1:14), which probably dealt with allegorical or fictitious interpretations of Old Testament genealogical lists. In reality, they were "doctrines of demons" (4:1), posing as God's truth (see 4:7).

7

the commandment (v. 5)—See verse 3, where the verb form "charge" is used (also in v. 8). The purpose of the charge in verses 3–4 is the spiritual virtue defined in verse 5. Timothy was to deliver this charge to the church. The goal of preaching the truth and warning of error is to call people to true salvation in Christ, which produces a love for God from a purified heart (2 Tim. 2:22; 1 Pet. 1:22), a cleansed conscience (Heb. 9:22; 10:14), and genuine faith (Heb. 10:22).

love (v. 5)—This is the love of choice and the will, characterized by self-denial and self-sacrifice for the benefit of others, and it is the mark of a true

5 *Now the purpose of the commandment is love from a pure heart, from a good conscience, and from sincere faith,*

6 *from which some, having strayed, have turned aside to idle talk,*

7 *desiring to be teachers of the law, understanding neither what they say nor the things which they affirm.*

8 *But we know that the law is good if one uses it lawfully,*

9 *knowing this: that the law is not made for a righteous person, but for the lawless and insubordinate, for the ungodly and for sinners, for the unholy and profane, for murderers of fathers and murderers of mothers, for manslayers,*

Christian (John 13:35; 1 John 4:7–8). In contrast, false doctrine produces only conflict and resulting "disputes" (vv. 4; 6:3–5).

good conscience (v. 5)—The Greek word for "good" refers to that which is perfect and produces pleasure and satisfaction. God created man with a "conscience" as his self-judging faculty. Because God has written His law on man's heart, man knows the basic standard of right and wrong. When he violates that standard, his conscience produces guilt, which acts as the mind's security system and produces fear, guilt, shame, and doubt as warnings of threats to the soul's well-being (see John 8:9; 1 Cor. 8:7, 10–12; Titus 1:15). On the other hand, when a believer does God's will, he enjoys the affirmation, assurance, peace, and joy of a good conscience (see Acts 23:1; 24:16; 2 Tim. 1:3; Heb. 13:18).

idle talk (v. 6)—This refers to speech that is aimless and has no logical end. It is essentially irrelevant and will not accomplish anything spiritual or edifying to believers. It can also be translated "fruitless discussion." False doctrine leads nowhere but to the deadening end of human speculation and demonic deception (see 6:3–5).

desiring to be teachers (v. 7)—The false teachers wanted the kind of prestige enjoyed by Jewish rabbis; but they were not concerned at all about truly learning the law and teaching it to others (see 6:4; Matt. 23:5–7). Instead, they imposed on believers in Ephesus a legalistic heresy that offered salvation by works.

not made for a righteous person (v. 9)—Those who think they are righteous will never be saved (Luke 5:32) because they do not understand the true purpose of the law. The false teachers, with their works system of personally achieved self-righteousness (in their own minds), had shown clearly that they misunderstood the law completely. It was not a means to self-righteousness, but a means to self-condemnation, sin, conviction, repentance, and pleading to God for mercy (v. 15).

lawless . . . profane (v. 9)—These first six characteristics, expressed in three couplets, delineate sins from the first half of the Ten Commandments, which deal with a person's relationship to God. "Lawless" describes those who have no commitment to any law or standard, which makes such people "insubordinate" or rebellious. Those who are "ungodly" have no regard for anything sacred, which means they are "sinners" because they disregard God's law. "Unholy" people are indifferent to what is right, which leads them to be the "profane," those who step on or trample what is sacred (see Heb. 10:29).

murderers of fathers . . . perjurers (vv. 9–10)—These sins are violations of the second half of the Ten Commandments—those dealing with relationships among people. These specific sins undoubtedly

10 *for fornicators, for sodomites, for kidnappers, for liars, for perjurers, and if there is any other thing that is contrary to sound doctrine,*

11 *according to the glorious gospel of the blessed God which was committed to my trust.*

12 *And I thank Christ Jesus our Lord who has enabled me, because He counted me faithful, putting me into the ministry,*

13 *although I was formerly a blasphemer, a persecutor, and an insolent man; but I obtained mercy because I did it ignorantly in unbelief.*

14 *And the grace of our Lord was exceedingly abundant, with faith and love which are in Christ Jesus.*

characterized the false teachers, since they are characteristic behaviors related to false doctrine (v. 10). "Murderers of fathers" and "mothers" is a violation of the Fifth Commandment (Exod. 20:12; see 21:15–17), which forbids everything from dishonor to murder. "Manslayers" (or "murderers") is in violation of the Sixth Commandment (Exod. 20:13). "Fornicators" and "sodomites" (or "homosexuals") violate the Seventh Commandment (Exod. 20:14), which prohibits sexual activity outside the marriage bed. Because the theft of children was commonplace in Paul's day, he mentions "kidnappers" in connection with the Eighth Commandment (Exod. 20:15), which prohibits stealing. Finally, "liars" and "perjurers" are violators of the Ninth Commandment (Exod. 20:16).

sound doctrine (v. 10)—This is a familiar emphasis in the Pastoral Epistles (see 2 Tim. 4:3; Titus 2:1). "Sound" refers to that which is healthy and wholesome. It is the kind of teaching that produces spiritual life and growth, which implies that false doctrine produces spiritual disease and debilitation.

the glorious gospel (v. 11)—The gospel reveals God's glory; that is, the perfections of His person or His attributes, including His holiness (hatred of sin) and justice (demand of punishment for violations of His law) and grace (forgiveness of sin). Those particular attributes are key to any effective gospel presentation.

committed (v. 11)—This Greek word refers to committing something of value to another and can be translated "entrusted." God entrusted Paul with the communication and guardianship of His revealed truth. (see 2:7; 6:20–21; Rom. 15:15–16; 1 Cor. 4:1–2; 9:17; 2 Cor. 5:18–20; Gal. 2:7; Col. 1:25; 1 Thess. 2:4).

counted me faithful (v. 12)—God's sovereign purpose for Paul and for all believers works through personal faith. Until Paul was turned by the Holy Spirit from self-righteous works (see Phil. 3:4–7) to faith alone in Christ, he could not be used by God. He was in the same condition as the useless false teachers (vv. 6–7).

a blasphemer, a persecutor, and an insolent man (v. 13)—This verse indicates that experience of Paul when he saw himself, in the light of God's law, for who he really was (see notes on Rom. 7:7–12). A "blasphemer" speaks evil of and slanders God. Paul violated the first half of the Ten Commandments through his overt attacks against Christ (see Acts 9:4–5; 22:7–8; 26:9, 14–15). As a "persecutor" and an "insolent man," Paul violated the second half through his attacks on believers. The Greek word for "insolent man" can be translated "violent aggressor," indicating the violence Paul heaped on Christians (see v. 20).

because I did it ignorantly in unbelief (v. 13)—Paul was neither a Jewish apostate nor a Pharisee who clearly understood Jesus' teaching and still rejected Him. He was a zealous, fastidious Jew trying to earn his salvation, thus lost and damned. His plea of ignorance was not a claim to innocence nor an excuse denying his guilt. It was simply a statement indicating that he did not understand the truth of Christ's gospel and was honestly trying to protect his religion. His willing repentance when confronted by Christ (see Rom. 7:9; Phil. 3:8–9) is evidence that he had not understood the ramifications of his actions—he truly thought he was doing God a service (Acts 26:9).

grace (v. 14)—God's loving forgiveness, by which He grants salvation apart from any merit on the part of those He saves (see notes on Rom. 3:24; Gal. 1:6)

faith and love (v. 14)—attitudes frequently linked with salvation in the New Testament (see Eph. 1:15; 3:17; Col. 1:4, 23). They are gifts of God's grace in Christ.

This is a faithful saying (v. 15)—A phrase unique to the Pastoral Epistles (see 3:1; 4:9; 2 Tim. 2:11; Titus 3:8), which announces a statement summarizing key doctrines. The phrase "worthy of all acceptance" gives the statement added emphasis. Apparently, these sayings were well known in the churches as concise expressions of cardinal gospel truth.

to save sinners (v. 15)—This faithful saying was based on the statements of Jesus recorded in Matthew 9:13.

I am chief (v. 15)—This is literally "first," in rank. Few could be considered a worse sinner than someone who blasphemed God and persecuted His church (see 1 Cor. 15:9; Eph. 3:8). Paul's attitude toward himself dramatically changed (see Phil. 3:7–9; Rom. 7:7–12).

for this reason (v. 16)—Paul was saved so that God could display His gracious and merciful patience with the most wretched sinners.

15 This is a faithful saying and worthy of all acceptance, that Christ Jesus came into the world to save sinners, of whom I am chief.

16 However, for this reason I obtained mercy, that in me first Jesus Christ might show all longsuffering, as a pattern to those who are going to believe on Him for everlasting life.

17 Now to the King eternal, immortal, invisible, to God who alone is wise, be honor and glory forever and ever. Amen.

18 This charge I commit to you, son Timothy, according to the prophecies previously made concerning you, that by them you may wage the good warfare,

19 having faith and a good conscience, which some having rejected, concerning the faith have suffered shipwreck,

20 of whom are Hymenaeus and Alexander, whom I delivered to Satan that they may learn not to blaspheme.

longsuffering (v. 16)—refers to patience with people

a pattern (v. 16)—This refers to a model or example. Paul was living proof that God could save any sinner, no matter how bad he might be. The account of Paul's conversion has been instrumental in the salvation of many. Paul's testimony is repeated six other times in the New Testament (Acts 9, 22, 26; Gal. 1–2; Phil. 3:1–14).

prophecies previously made concerning you (v. 18)—The Greek word for "previously made" literally means "leading the way to," implying that a series of prophecies had been given about Timothy in connection with his receiving his spiritual gift. These prophecies specifically and supernaturally called Timothy into God's service.

wage the good warfare (v. 18)—Paul urged Timothy to fight the battle against the enemies of Christ and the gospel.

faith . . . faith (v. 19)—The first is subjective and means continuing to believe the truth. The second is objective, referring to the content of the Christian gospel.

shipwreck (v. 19)—A good conscience serves as the rudder that steers the believer through the rocks and reefs of sin and error. The false teachers ignored their consciences and the truth, and as a result, suffered shipwreck of the Christian faith (the true doctrine of the gospel), which implies severe spiritual catastrophe. This does not imply loss of salvation of a true believer (see notes on Rom. 8:31–39) but likely indicates the tragic loss that comes to the apostate. They had been in the church, heard the gospel, and rejected it in favor of the false doctrine defined in verses 3–7. Apostasy is a turning away from the gospel, having once claimed to accept it (see notes on Heb. 2:3–4; 3:12–15; 10:26–31).

Hymenaeus and Alexander (v. 20)—Hymenaeus is mentioned in 2 Timothy 2:17 in connection with Philetus, another false teacher. Alexander may be the opponent of the faith referred to in 2 Timothy 4:14–15. Nothing else is known about these two men.

I delivered to Satan (v. 20)—Paul put both men out of the church, thus ending their influence and removing them from the protection and insulation of God's people. They were no longer in the environment of God's blessing, but under Satan's control. In some instances God has turned believers over to Satan for positive purposes, such as revealing the genuineness of saving faith, keeping them humble and dependent on Him, enabling them to strengthen others, or offering God praise (see Job 1:1–22; Rev. 7:9–15). God hands some people over to Satan for judgment, such as King Saul (1 Sam. 16:12–16; 28:4–20), Judas (John 13:27), and the sinning member in the Corinthian church (see 1 Cor. 5:1–5).

may learn not to blaspheme (v. 20)—Paul learned not to blaspheme when confronted by the true understanding of the law and the gospel. That was what those men needed. God, the inspired text seems to indicate, would teach them and show them grace as he had Paul. But that evangelistic work could not go on at the expense of the purity of the church.

1) What specific instructions does Paul give Timothy regarding false teachers?

_____

_____

_____

_____

(Verses to consider: 2 Cor. 2:17; Titus 1:10–11)

2) In what way does Paul describe what the false teachers had done (vv. 4–7, 19)?

_____

_____

_____

_____

3) What is the "glorious gospel" (v. 11)?

_____

_____

_____

_____

4) How does Paul's personal testimony relate to his warning against false teachers?

_____

_____

_____

_____

(Verses to consider: Acts 9:1–9; John 1:17; Rom. 1:5; 1 Cor. 15:9; Eph. 3:8)

5) What does Paul mean when he urges Timothy to "wage the good warfare" (v. 18)?

_____

_____

_____

GOING DEEPER

Paul wrote fervently to Timothy because he deeply loved the church at Ephesus and had been concerned about them for some time. For what Paul said to the leaders when he left Ephesus, read Acts 20:25–31.

25 *"And indeed, now I know that you all, among whom I have gone preaching the kingdom of God, will see my face no more.*

26 *Therefore I testify to you this day that I am innocent of the blood of all men.*

27 *For I have not shunned to declare to you the whole counsel of God.*

28 *Therefore take heed to yourselves and to all the flock, among which the Holy Spirit has made you overseers, to shepherd the church of God which He purchased with His own blood.*

29 *For I know this, that after my departure savage wolves will come in among you, not sparing the flock.*

30 *Also from among yourselves men will rise up, speaking perverse things, to draw away the disciples after themselves.*

31 *Therefore watch, and remember that for three years I did not cease to warn everyone night and day with tears.*

Exploring the Meaning

6) Summarize Paul's main concern when he left the leaders at Ephesus. What was his final advice?

_____

_____

_____

_____

_____

7) Read John 8:44. Who or what is the ultimate source of false doctrine?

_____

_____

_____

_____

(Verses to consider: 2 Cor. 11:13–14; 1 John 4:1)

8) Read Titus 1:15–16. What further insights does this related passage offer regarding false teachers?

_____

_____

_____

_____

Truth for Today

All believers have a responsibility to be on the alert for false teachers. What do we watch for? First, look at their understanding of Scripture, and ask if their teaching is biblically sound. Do they place extra-biblical teachings on a par with the Bible? Do they handle accurately the Word of truth (2 Tim. 2:15)?

Second, examine their goals. Do they seek to love, honor, and glorify God? Or do they pursue self-love, material wealth, or personal happiness? Does their message speak of purity of heart, a good conscience, and non-hypocritical faith?

Third, examine their motives. Are they humble and selfless? Or do they seek the preeminence?

Finally, examine the effect of their teaching. Did their followers understand clearly the gospel of Jesus Christ? Do they define the gospel properly? Do they use the law properly, as part of the gospel message, or do they promote works righteousness?

Those who pass the above checks should be welcomed as brothers in Christ, even if we differ with them at some points of interpretation or doctrine. Those who do not are to be rejected, no matter what experiences they may have had, or what else they may teach. Constant vigilance is our defense against those who would enslave all of us to a false gospel.

REFLECTING ON THE TEXT

9) Paul considered Timothy a "son" and discipled and mentored him in the faith. Who in your life could serve as a "Paul" to you? Who can you take under your wing as a "Timothy"?

_____

_____

_____

_____

10) What specific changes do you need to make in your daily life to live with "a good conscience"?

_____

_____

_____

_____

11) Think about your own salvation story. How can you use your experience to encourage others this week?

_____

_____

_____

_____

Personal Response

Write out additional reflections, questions you may have, or a prayer.

_____

_____

_____

_____

_____

_____

_____

_____

_____

_____

_____

_____

_____

_____

_____

_____

_____

_____

_____

_____

_____

_____

_____

_____

_____

_____

ADDITIONAL NOTES

THE IMPORTANCE OF PRAYER

DRAWING NEAR

When has your prayer life been most vibrant? To what do you attribute this?

_____

_____

_____

_____

Do you think prayer really changes things? Why?

_____

_____

_____

_____

THE CONTEXT

The Ephesian church may have become lax in praying for the lost since Paul urged Timothy to make it a priority again. The Judaistic false teachers in Ephesus, by a perverted gospel and the teaching that salvation was only for Jews and Gentile proselytes to Judaism, would have certainly restricted evangelistic praying—interceding for the salvation of others. Their religious exclusivism (salvation only for the elite) would preclude the need for prayer for the lost.

The fact that Paul begins his discourse on church affairs with this particular topic indicates the important role that prayer is to play in the life of the church. If God's primary objective for His church involved fellowship, knowledge of the Scriptures, or conformity to the image of Christ, His plan would be best accomplished by bringing us to heaven immediately. But these are not the central functions of the church on earth. God has left us here to reach the lost. And before the church carries out this mission in the world, it must first grasp the breadth of the gospel call. This requires coming to terms with evangelistic praying. This particular passage calls for Christians to intercede for the lost in general. Furthermore, it raises the question of whether God hears such prayers, as well as what part they play in God's eternal plan.

KEYS TO THE TEXT

Supplications and Intercessions: Paul mentions two types of prayers. The Greek word for "supplication" comes from a root word that means "to lack," "to be deprived," or "to be without." Thus this kind of prayer occurs because of a need. The lost have a great need for salvation, and believers should ask God to meet that need. This word "intercession" comes from a root word meaning "to fall in with someone" or "to draw near so as to speak intimately." The verb from which this word derives is used of Christ's and the Spirit's intercession for believers (Rom. 8:26; Heb. 7:25). Paul desires the Ephesian Christians to have compassion for the lost, to understand the depths of their pain and misery, and to come intimately to God pleading for their salvation.

Ransom: This describes the result of Christ's substitutionary death for believers—which He did voluntarily (John 10:17–18)—and reminds us of Christ's own statement in Matthew 20:28 that He would be "a ransom for many." Not all will be ransomed (though His death would be sufficient), but only the many who believe by the work of the Holy Spirit and for whom the actual atonement was made. Christ did not pay a ransom only; He became the object of God's just wrath in the believer's place—He died his death and bore his sin (see 2 Cor. 5:21; 1 Pet. 2:24).

UNLEASHING THE TEXT

Read 2:1–8, noting the key words and definitions next to the passage.

all men (v. 1)—The lost in general, not the elect only. God's decree of election is secret—believers have no way of knowing who is elect until they respond. The scope of God's evangelistic efforts is broader than election (Matt. 22:14; John 17:21, 23).

kings and all who are in authority (v. 2)—Because so many powerful and influential political rulers are hostile to God, they are often the targets of bitterness and animosity. But Paul urges believers to pray that these leaders might repent of their sins and embrace the gospel, which meant that the Ephesians were even to pray for the salvation of the Roman emperor, Nero, a cruel and vicious blasphemer and persecutor of the faith.

1 Timothy 2:1–8 (NKJV)

1 *Therefore I exhort first of all that supplications, prayers, intercessions, and giving of thanks be made for all men,*

2 *for kings and all who are in authority, that we may lead a quiet and peaceable life in all godliness and reverence.*

a quiet and peaceable life (v. 2)—"Quiet" refers to the absence of external disturbances; "peaceable" refers to the absence of internal ones. While it remains uncompromising in its commitment to the truth, the church is not to agitate or disrupt the national life. When it manifests love and goodness to all and prays passionately for the lost, including rulers, the church may experience a certain amount of religious freedom. Persecution should only be the result of righteous living, not civil disobedience (see Titus 3:1–4; 1 Pet. 2:13–23).

3 *For this is good and acceptable in the sight of God our Savior,*

4 *who desires all men to be saved and to come to the knowledge of the truth.*

5 *For there is one God and one Mediator between God and men, the Man Christ Jesus,*

6 *who gave Himself a ransom for all, to be testified in due time,*

7 *for which I was appointed a preacher and an apostle—I am speaking the truth in Christ and*

godliness and reverence (v. 2)—"Godliness" is a key word in this letter (3:16; 4:7–8; 6:3, 5–6, 11; see 2 Tim. 3:5; Titus 1:1), indicating that there needed to be a call back to holy living, which had been negatively affected by the false doctrine. Godliness refers to having the proper attitude and conduct before God in everything; "reverence" can be translated "moral earnestness," and refers to moral dignity and holy behavior before men.

desires all men to be saved (v. 4)—The Greek word for "desires" is not that which normally expresses God's will of decree (His eternal purpose), but God's will of desire. There is a distinction between God's desire and His eternal saving purpose, which must transcend His desires. God does not want people to sin. He hates sin with all His being (Ps. 5:4; 45:7); thus, He hates its consequences—eternal wickedness in hell. God does not want people to remain wicked forever in eternal remorse and hatred of Himself. Yet, God, for His own glory, and to manifest that glory in wrath, chose to endure "vessels . . . prepared for destruction" for the supreme fulfillment of His will (Rom. 9:22). In His eternal purpose, He chose only the elect out of the world (John 17:6) and passed over the rest, leaving them to the consequences of their sin, unbelief, and rejection of Christ. Ultimately, God's choices are determined by His sovereign, eternal purpose, not His desires.

the knowledge of the truth (v. 4)—meaning "to be saved"; see 2 Timothy 3:7

there is one God (v. 5)—There is no other way of salvation (Acts 4:12); hence there is the need to pray for the lost to come to know the one true God (see Deut. 4:35, 39; 6:4; Isa. 43:10; 44:6; 45:5–6, 21–22; 46:9; 1 Cor. 8:4, 6).

Mediator (v. 5)—This refers to someone who intervenes between two parties to resolve a conflict or ratify a covenant. Jesus Christ is the only "Mediator" who can restore peace between God and sinners (Heb. 8:6; 9:15; 12:24).

the Man Christ Jesus (v. 5)—The absence of the article before "Man" in the Greek suggests the translation "Christ Jesus, Himself a man." Only the perfect God-Man could bring God and man together (see Job 9:32–33).

for all (v. 6)—This should be taken in two senses: (1) there are temporal benefits of the atonement that accrue to all men universally (see 4:10), and (2) Christ's death was sufficient to cover the sins of all people. Yet the substitutionary aspect of His death is applied to the elect alone (see above and 2 Cor. 5:14–21). Christ's death is therefore unlimited in its sufficiency, but limited in its application. Because Christ's expiation of sin is indivisible, inexhaustible, and sufficient to cover the guilt of all the sins that will ever be committed, God can clearly offer it to all. Yet only the elect will respond and be saved, according to His eternal purpose (see John 17:12).

in due time (v. 6)—at the proper time in God's redemptive plan (see Gal. 4:4)

for which (v. 7)—Paul's divine commission was based on the truths delineated in verses 3–6.

preacher (v. 7)—The Greek word derives from the verb that means "to herald," "to proclaim," or "to speak publicly." Paul was a public herald proclaiming the gospel of Christ.

I am speaking the truth . . . not lying (v. 7)—Paul's emphatic outburst of his apostolic authority and integrity is to emphasize that he was a teacher of the Gentiles.

teacher of the Gentiles (v. 7)—This is the distinctive feature of Paul's apostolic appointment, which demonstrates the universal scope of the gospel. Paul's need to make this distinction suggests he was dealing with some form of Jewish exclusivism that had crippled the Ephesians' interest in praying for Gentiles to be saved.

> not lying—a teacher of the Gentiles in faith and truth.
>
> 8 I desire therefore that the men pray everywhere, lifting up holy hands, without wrath and doubting.

men (v. 8)—This is the Greek word for "men" as opposed to women. God intends for men to be the leaders when the church meets for corporate worship. When prayer for the lost is offered during those times, the men are to lead it.

everywhere (v. 8)—Paul's reference to the official assembly of the church (see 1 Cor. 1:2; 2 Cor. 2:14; 1 Thess. 1:8)

lifting up holy hands (v. 8)—Paul is not emphasizing a specific posture necessary for prayer, but a pre-requisite for effective prayer. Though this posture is described in the Old Testament, so are many others. The Greek word for "holy" means "unpolluted" or "unstained by evil." "Hands" symbolize the activities of life; thus "holy hands" represent a holy life. The basis of effective prayer is a righteous life (James 5:16).

without wrath and doubting (v. 8)—"Wrath" and righteousness are mutually exclusive (James 1:20; see Luke 9:52–56). A better translation for "doubting" is "dissension," and it refers to a hesitant reluctance to be committed to prayer. "Effectual, fervent" prayer is effective (James 5:16). The two refer to one's inner attitude.

1) For whom did Paul command prayers to be made?

_____

_____

_____

2) What reasons are given for these commands to "pray for all men"?

_____

_____

_____

3) What is significant about the command to pray "lifting up holy hands" (v. 8)?

_____

_____

_____

(Verses to consider: 1 Kings 8:22; Neh. 8:6; Ps. 28:2; 63:4; 134:2)

Going Deeper

Paul encouraged Timothy to pray for all people. For insight into what Jesus said about prayer, read Matthew 6:5–15.

5 *"And when you pray, you shall not be like the hypocrites. For they love to pray standing in the synagogues and on the corners of the streets, that they may be seen by men. Assuredly, I say to you, they have their reward.*

6 *But you, when you pray, go into your room, and when you have shut your door, pray to your Father who is in the secret place; and your Father who sees in secret will reward you openly.*

7 *And when you pray, do not use vain repetitions as the heathen do. For they think that they will be heard for their many words.*

8 *"Therefore do not be like them. For your Father knows the things you have need of before you ask Him.*

9 *In this manner, therefore, pray: Our Father in heaven, hallowed be Your name.*

10 *Your kingdom come. Your will be done on earth as it is in heaven.*

11 *Give us this day our daily bread.*

12 *And forgive us our debts, as we forgive our debtors.*

13 *And do not lead us into temptation, but deliver us from the evil one. For Yours is the kingdom and the power and the glory forever. Amen.*

14 *"For if you forgive men their trespasses, your heavenly Father will also forgive you.*

15 *But if you do not forgive men their trespasses, neither will your Father forgive your trespasses.*

Exploring the Meaning

4) What is Jesus' main point in verses 5–8?

_____

_____

_____

_____

5) What part does forgiveness play in our prayer life?

_____

_____

_____

6) How does this teaching on prayer compare with what you discovered in 1 Timothy 2:1–8?

_____

_____

_____

_____

_____

7) What does Paul's command to pray for all people imply? Will everyone be saved? (See Eph. 1:3–5).

_____

_____

_____

_____

_____

(Verses to consider: Rom. 1:18–32; 9:22–23)

TRUTH FOR TODAY

The greatest example of evangelistic praying is our Lord Himself. Isaiah 53:12 tells us He "interceded for the transgressors." On the cross He prayed, "Father, forgive them; for they do not know what they are doing" (Luke 23:34). God answered those prayers with three thousand converts on the Day of Pentecost, and countless thousands more through the centuries.

Do we pray for the lost like that? Do we have the passion that inspired John Knox to cry out, "Give me Scotland or I die"? Is our attitude that of George Whitefield, who prayed, "O Lord, give me souls or take my soul"? Can we, like Henry Martyn, say, "I cannot endure existence if Jesus is to be so dishonored"?

God honors evangelistic prayer. Standing among those who killed Stephen was a young man named Saul of Tarsus. Could it be that the great apostle's salvation was in answer to Stephen's prayer, "Lord, do not hold this sin against them"? Evangelism begins with the evangelistic prayer.

REFLECTING ON THE TEXT

8) List five prominent figures who have great influence in our culture. How might God use your faithful prayers to change them (and the world through them)? How can you pray for them?

_____

_____

_____

_____

9) If every Christian in your church imitated your personal prayer habits, how much prayer would be taking place? What, if anything, needs to change in your prayer life?

_____

_____

_____

_____

_____

PERSONAL RESPONSE

Write out additional reflections, questions you may have, or a prayer.

_____

_____

_____

_____

_____

_____

_____

_____

_____

Additional Notes

_____

_____

_____

_____

_____

_____

_____

_____

_____

_____

_____

_____

_____

_____

_____

_____

_____

_____

_____

_____

_____

_____

_____

_____

_____

_____

_____

_____

_____

_____

3

THE ROLE OF WOMEN

DRAWING NEAR

How would you answer a skeptic's charge that Christianity is demeaning to women?

_____

_____

_____

What women, in your church or other spheres, do you greatly admire? Why?

_____

_____

_____

THE CONTEXT

Few topics are as hotly debated as the subject of the role of women in the church. Sadly, this debate no longer looks to the pages of God's Word in order to find a solution. Long-held beliefs are being abandoned in favor of new and culturally acceptable feminist doctrines. Churches, schools, and seminaries are increasingly jettisoning the bedrock truths upon which they were founded. Countless books continue to be written which articulate and defend these new views concerning the role of women in the church. Ironically, many of these same authors once held the traditional, biblical view. But due to the pressure of feminism, these church leaders have sacrificed biblical integrity for cultural acceptance. The Bible passages that clearly delineate women's roles are constantly reinterpreted, or else they are ignored because of the supposed "anti-woman bias" of the biblical writers.

Since the church at Ephesus was overrun with false teachers, it is not surprising to discover that they also wrestled with the issue of gender roles. Apparently, some of the women in the church were leading lives of impurity (see 5:6, 11–15; 2 Tim. 3:6), and their inappropriate behavior carried over into the worship services of the church. Under the guise of coming together to worship, these women were calling attention to themselves and proving to be a serious distraction to the rest of the body. Since worship is central to the life of the church, Paul confronted the issue immediately in his letter to Timothy.

Contrary to much popular belief, this passage is as culturally relevant as any other New Testament passage.

KEYS TO THE TEXT

Silence and Submission: "Silence" ("quiet") and "submission" ("to line up under") were to characterize the role of a woman as a learner in the context of the church assembly. Paul explains his meaning in verse 12: Women are to be silent by not teaching, and they are to demonstrate submission by not usurping the authority of the pastors or elders. Elsewhere Paul says that *every* spirit-filled Christian is to be a humble, submissive Christian (Eph. 5:21). No believer is inherently superior to any other believer. In their standing before God, they are equal in every way (Gal. 3:28). All believers are to submit to each other. Wives are to submit to their husbands, and children are to submit to their parents (Eph. 6:1–3). Believers must submit to government laws and ordinances (Rom. 13:1; 1 Pet. 2:13). Younger men should submit to older men (1 Pet. 5:5a). God desires *every* believer to be submissive in the ways He has ordained.

Woman's Role from Creation: A woman's subordinate role did not result after the Fall as a cultural, chauvinistic corruption of God's perfect design; rather, God established her role as part of His original creation (1 Tim. 2:13). God made woman after man to be his suitable helper (see 1 Cor. 11:8–9). The Fall actually corroborates God's divine plan of creation (see Gen. 3:1–7). By nature Eve was not suited to assume the position of ultimate responsibility. By leaving Adam's protection and usurping his headship, she was vulnerable and fell, thus confirming how important it was for her to stay under the protection and leadership of her husband (see 5:11–12; 2 Tim. 3:6–7). Adam then violated his leadership role, followed Eve in her sin, and plunged the human race into sinfulness—all connected with violating God's planned roles for the sexes. Ultimately, the responsibility for the Fall rests with Adam, since he chose to disobey God by being deceived.

UNLEASHING THE TEXT

Read 2:9–15, noting the key words and definitions next to the passage.

26

1 Timothy 2:9–15 (NKJV)

9 *In like manner also, that the women adorn themselves in modest apparel, with propriety and moderation, not with braided hair or gold or pearls or costly clothing,*

10 *but, which is proper for women professing godliness, with good works.*

11 *Let a woman learn in silence with all submission.*

12 *And I do not permit a woman to teach or to have authority over a man, but to be in silence.*

13 *For Adam was formed first, then Eve.*

14 *And Adam was not deceived, but the woman being deceived, fell into transgression.*

15 *Nevertheless she will be saved in childbearing if they continue in faith, love, and holiness, with self-control.*

adorn . . . modest apparel (v. 9)—The Greek word for "adorn" means "to arrange," "to put in order," or "to make ready." A woman is to arrange herself appropriately for the worship service, which includes wearing decent clothing that reflects a properly adorned, chaste heart.

propriety and moderation (v. 9)—The Greek word for "propriety" refers to modesty mixed with humility, which carries the underlying idea of shame. It can also refer to a rejection of anything dishonorable to God, or refer to grief over sin. "Moderation" basically refers to self-control over sexual passions. Godly women hate sin and control their passions so as not to lead another into sin.

braided hair or gold or pearls or costly clothing (v. 9)—These specific practices were causing distraction and discord in the church. Women in the first century often wove gold, pearls or other jewelry into their hair styles ("braided hair") to call attention to themselves and their wealth or beauty. The same was true of those women who wore "costly clothing." By doing so they would draw attention to themselves and away from the Lord, likely causing the poorer women to be envious. Paul's point was to forbid the preoccupation of certain women with flaunting their wealth and distracting people from worshiping the Lord.

Let a woman learn (v. 11)—Women are not to be the public teachers when the church assembles, but neither are they to be shut out of the learning process. The form of the Greek verb translated "let . . . learn" is an imperative: Paul is commanding that women be taught in the church. That was a novel concept, since neither first-century Judaism nor Greek culture held women in high esteem. Some of the women in Ephesus probably overreacted to the cultural denigration they had typically suffered and took advantage of their opportunity in the church by seeking a dominant role in leadership.

I do not permit (v. 12)—The Greek word for "permit" is used in the New Testament to refer to allowing someone to do what he desires. Paul may have been addressing a real situation in which several women in Ephesus desired to be public preachers.

to teach (v. 12)—Paul used a verbal form of this Greek word that indicates a condition or process and is better translated "to be a teacher." This was an important, official function in the church. Thus Paul is forbidding women from filling the office and role of the pastor or teacher. He is not prohibiting them from teaching in other appropriate conditions and circumstances.

to have authority over (v. 12)—Paul forbids women from exercising any type of authority over men in the church assembly, since the elders are those who rule (5:17). The elders are all to be men (as is clear from the requirements in 3:2, 5).

she (v. 15)—That Paul does not have Eve in mind here is clear because the verb translated "will be saved" is future, and he also uses the plural pronoun "they." He is talking about women after Eve.

will be saved (v. 15)—In this context this is better translated "will be preserved." The Greek word can also mean "to rescue," "to preserve safe and unharmed," "to heal," or "to deliver from." It appears several times in the New Testament without reference to spiritual salvation (see Matt. 8:25; 9:21–22; 24:22; 27:40, 42, 49; 2 Tim. 4:18). Paul is not advocating that women are eternally saved from sin through childbearing or that they maintain their salvation by having babies, both of which would be clear contradictions of the New Testament teaching of salvation by grace alone through faith alone (Rom. 3:19–20) which is sustained forever (Rom. 8:31–39). Paul is teaching that even though a woman bears the stigma of being the initial instrument who led the race into sin, women may be preserved or freed from that stigma by raising a generation of godly children (see 5:10).

in childbearing (v. 15)—Because mothers have a unique bond and intimacy with their children and spend far more time with them than do fathers, they have far greater influence in their lives and thus a unique responsibility and opportunity for rearing godly children. While a woman may have led the human race into sin, women have the privilege of leading many out of sin to godliness. Paul is speaking in general terms; God does not want all women to be married, let alone bear children.

if they continue in faith, love, and holiness, with self-control (v. 15)—The godly appearance, demeanor, and behavior commanded of believing women in the church (vv. 9–12) is motivated by the promise of deliverance from any inferior status and the joy of raising godly children.

1) What instructions concerning dress did Paul give to Timothy for the women in his congregation?

_____

_____

_____

_____

_____

(Verses to consider: Gen. 24:53; Isa. 3:16–24; Prov. 31:22; 1 Pet. 3:3–4)

2) What behavior is expected from women professing godliness, and what is their God-ordained role in the church? What vitally important role do they play in the home?

_____

_____

_____

_____

_____

(Verses to consider: 1 Cor. 14:34–35; Titus 2:3–5)

3) Summarize what this passage says about God's design for women from creation (vv. 13–14)?

_____

_____

_____

_____

_____

(Verses to consider: Gen. 2:18; 3:1–7)

GOING DEEPER

In his book to the church at Corinth, Paul related the theological foundation for his teaching on women's roles. Read 1 Corinthians 11:1–16.

1   *Imitate me, just as I also imitate Christ.*
2   *Now I praise you, brethren, that you remember me in all things and keep the traditions just as I delivered them to you.*
3   *But I want you to know that the head of every man is Christ, the head of woman is man, and the head of Christ is God.*
4   *Every man praying or prophesying, having his head covered, dishonors his head.*
5   *But every woman who prays or prophesies with her head uncovered dishonors her head, for that is one and the same as if her head were shaved.*
6   *For if a woman is not covered, let her also be shorn. But if it is shameful for a woman to be shorn or shaved, let her be covered.*
7   *For a man indeed ought not to cover his head, since he is the image and glory of God; but woman is the glory of man.*
8   *For man is not from woman, but woman from man.*
9   *Nor was man created for the woman, but woman for the man.*
10 *For this reason the woman ought to have a symbol of authority on her head, because of the angels.*
11 *Nevertheless, neither is man independent of woman, nor woman independent of man, in the Lord.*
12 *For as woman came from man, even so man also comes through woman; but all things are from God.*
13 *Judge among yourselves. Is it proper for a woman to pray to God with her head uncovered?*

29

14 *Does not even nature itself teach you that if a man has long hair, it is a dishonor to him?*

15 *But if a woman has long hair, it is a glory to her; for her hair is given to her for a covering.*

16 *But if anyone seems to be contentious, we have no such custom, nor do the churches of God.*

EXPLORING THE MEANING

4) What does this passage mean when it discusses "headship"?

_____

_____

_____

_____

5) Read Galatians 3:28. How does this verse put to rest any notion that Christianity views men as superior to women?

_____

_____

_____

_____

6) Read Luke 8:2–3. How did Jesus give honor to women during His earthly ministry?

_____

_____

_____

_____

(Verses to consider: Mark 5:25–34; Luke 10:38–42; 13:11–13; John 4:1–30)

TRUTH FOR TODAY

God has perfectly balanced the roles of the sexes. Men are to be the leaders in the church and the family. Women are kept from any accusation of inferiority through the godly influence they have in the lives of their precious children. For the church to depart from this divine order is to perpetuate the disaster of the Fall.

Reflecting on the Text

7) How do you feel about Paul's teaching about women in this passage? Why?

_____

_____

_____

_____

_____

8) What does it mean for men and women to dress appropriately?

_____

_____

_____

_____

9) If you are a woman, how can you modify your habits of dress to better conform to the commands in this passage? How can you modify your heart and attitude to do the same?

_____

_____

_____

_____

10) What criticism can a church expect if it preaches and enacts the principles taught in this passage? How do you know?

_____

_____

_____

_____

11) What godly woman (or women) has God used in your life to help you grow in the faith? How can you show appreciation this week for that spiritual investment?

_____

_____

_____

_____

_____

PERSONAL RESPONSE

Write out additional reflections, questions you may have, or a prayer.

_____

_____

_____

_____

_____

_____

_____

_____

_____

_____

_____

_____

_____

_____

_____

4

QUALIFICATIONS FOR LEADERSHIP

DRAWING NEAR

Paul moves to the business of running a church. Of primary importance to any church is that its leaders set an example for the flock. On a scale of 1–10 (1 = "terrible"; 10 = "terrific"), how would you rate your church leaders in this area?

_____

_____

_____

What attributes does our society generally view as indispensable for leadership?

_____

_____

_____

_____

In your opinion, what are the marks of a good leader?

_____

_____

_____

_____

THE CONTEXT

Paul's purpose in writing this letter was to instruct Timothy regarding the church. Clearly, there is an inseparable link between the spiritual quality of a congregation and the godliness of its leaders. Not surprisingly, church leadership is a major focus of teaching in the New Testament. This passage delineates those qualifications for pastors and deacons.

The qualifications given by the Spirit stand in sharp contrast to the unqualified leaders that had assumed positions in the church at Ephesus. The epistle indicates the presence of some leaders who were propagating false doctrine (1:3; 4:1–3, 7; 6:3–5). They overemphasized the law and twisted the gospel (1:7–11). Also, certain women had wrongly assumed power. All needed to be publicly rebuked.

Rather than emphasize the duties of elders and deacons, Paul emphasized the character qualities that should mark a leader of God's church. The duties of church leaders were evident, but the individual qualifications needed clarification.

KEYS TO THE TEXT

Bishop: The word means "over" and identifies the men who are responsible to lead the church. The New Testament uses the words "bishop," "elder," "overseer," and "pastor" interchangeably to describe the same men. Bishops (pastors, overseers, elders) are responsible to lead, preach, teach, help the spiritually weak, care for the church, and ordain other leaders.

Deacons: This word comes from a word group meaning "to serve," and originally referred to menial tasks such as waiting on tables (see Acts 6:1–4). "Deacon" came to denote any service in the church. Deacons serve under the leadership of elders, helping them exercise oversight in the practical matters of church life. Scripture defines no official or specific responsibilities for deacons; they are to do whatever the elders assign them or whatever spiritual ministry is necessary.

UNLEASHING THE TEXT

Read 3:1–16, noting the key words and definitions next to the passage.

1 Timothy 3:1–16 (NKJV)

desires . . . desires (v. 1)—Two different Greek words are used. The first means "to reach out after." It describes external action, not internal motive. The second means "a strong passion," and refers to an inward desire. Taken together, these two words aptly describe the type of man who belongs in the ministry—one who outwardly pursues it because he is driven by a strong internal desire.

1 This is a faithful saying: If a man desires the position of a bishop, he desires a good work.

2 A bishop then must be blameless, the husband of one wife, temperate, sober-minded, of good behavior, hospitable, able to teach;

must (v. 2)—The use of this Greek particle stresses emphatically that living a blameless life is absolutely necessary for church leaders.

blameless (v. 2)—This means literally "not able to be held" in a criminal sense; there is no valid accusation of wrongdoing that can be made against him. No overt, flagrant sin can mar the life of one who must be an example for his people to follow (see v. 10; 4:16; 5:7; Ps. 101:6; 2 Thess. 3:9; Heb. 13:7; 1 Pet. 5:3). This is the over-arching requirement for elders; the rest of the qualifications elaborate on what it means to be blameless.

3 *not given to wine, not violent, not greedy for money, but gentle, not quarrelsome, not covetous;*

the husband of one wife (v. 2)—In Greek, this is literally a "one-woman man." This says nothing about marriage or divorce (for comments on that, see note on v. 4). The issue is not the elder's marital status, but his moral and sexual purity. This qualification heads the list, because it is in this area that leaders are most prone to fail. Various interpretations of this qualification have been offered. Some see it as a prohibition against polygamy—an unnecessary injunction since polygamy was not common in Roman society and clearly forbidden by Scripture (Gen. 2:24), the teaching of Jesus (Matt. 19:5–6; Mark 10:6–9), and Paul (Eph. 5:31). A polygamist could not even have been a church member, let alone a church leader. Others see this requirement as barring those who remarried after the death of their wives. But, as already noted, the issue is sexual purity, not marital status. Further, the Bible encourages remarriage after widowhood (5:14; 1 Cor. 7:39). Some believe that Paul here excludes divorced men from church leadership. That again ignores the fact that this qualification does not deal with marital status. Nor does the Bible prohibit all remarriage after divorce (see Matt. 5:31–32; 19:9; 1 Cor. 7:15). Finally, some think that this requirement excludes single men from church leadership. But if that were Paul's intent, he would have disqualified himself (1 Cor. 7:8). A "one-woman man" is one totally devoted to his wife, maintaining singular devotion, affection, and sexual purity in both thought and deed. To violate this is to forfeit blamelessness and no longer be "above reproach" (Titus 1:6–7).

temperate (v. 2)—The Greek word literally means "wineless" but is here used metaphorically to mean "alert," "watchful," "vigilant," or "clear-headed." Elders must be able to think clearly.

sober-minded (v. 2)—A "sober-minded" man is disciplined, knows how to properly order his priorities, and is serious about spiritual matters.

good behavior (v. 2)—The Greek word means "orderly." Elders must not lead chaotic lives. If they cannot order their own lives, how can they bring order to the church?

hospitable (v. 2)—This comes from a compound Greek word meaning "love of strangers" (see Heb. 13:2). As with all spiritual virtues, elders must set the example; their lives and homes are to be open so all can see their spiritual character.

able to teach (v. 2)—This is used only here and in 2 Timothy 2:24. This is the only qualification relating to an elder's giftedness and spiritual ability, and the only one that distinguishes elders from deacons. The preaching and teaching of God's Word is the over/pastor/elder's primary duty (4:6, 11, 13; 5:17).

not given to wine (v. 3)—This is more than a mere prohibition against drunkenness (see Eph. 5:18). An elder must not have a reputation as a drinker; his judgment must never be clouded by alcohol (see Prov. 31:4–5), and his lifestyle must be radically different from the world and lead others to holiness, not sin.

not violent (v. 3)—Literally "not a giver of blows," this means that elders must react to difficult situations calmly and gently, and under no circumstances with physical violence.

not greedy for money (v. 3)—The better Greek manuscripts omit this phrase. See the note below on "not covetous." The principle is included, however, in Titus 1:7 and 1 Peter 5:2.

gentle (v. 3)—considerate, genial, gracious, quick to pardon failure, and one who does not hold a grudge

not quarrelsome (v. 3)—"peaceful," "reluctant to fight"; one who does not promote disunity or disharmony

not covetous (v. 3)—Elders must be motivated by love for God and His people, not money (see 1 Pet. 5:2). A leader who is in the ministry for money reveals a heart set on the world, not the things of God. Covetousness characterizes false teachers (Titus 1:11; 2 Pet. 2:1–3, 14; Jude 11), but not Paul's ministry (Acts 20:33; 1 Cor. 9:1–16; 2 Cor. 11:9; 1 Thess. 2:5).

who rules his own house well
(v. 4)—The elder's home life, like his personal life, must be exemplary. He must be one who "rules" (presides over, has authority over) "his own house" (everything connected with his home, not merely his wife and children) "well" (intrinsically good; excellently). Issues of divorce should be related to this matter. A divorced man gives no evidence of a well-managed home, but rather that divorce shows weakness in his spiritual leadership. If there has been a biblically permitted divorce, it must have been so far in the past as to have been overcome by a long pattern of solid family leadership and the rearing of godly children.

4 one who rules his own house well, having his children in submission with all reverence

5 (for if a man does not know how to rule his own house, how will he take care of the church of God?);

6 not a novice, lest being puffed up with pride he fall into the same condemnation as the devil.

7 Moreover he must have a good testimony among those who are outside, lest he fall into reproach and the snare of the devil.

8 Likewise deacons must be reverent, not double-tongued, not given to much wine, not greedy for money,

9 holding the mystery of the faith with a pure conscience.

submission (v. 4)—This is a military term referring to soldiers ranked under one in authority. An elder's children must be believers (see note on "faithful" in Titus 1:6), well-behaved, and respectful.

take care of the church of God (v. 5)—An elder must first prove in the intimacy and exposure of his own home his ability to lead others to salvation and sanctification. There he proves God has gifted him to set the example of virtue, serve others, resolve conflicts, build unity, and maintain love. If he cannot do those essential things there, why would anyone assume he would be able to do them in the church?

not a novice, lest . . . puffed up with pride (v. 6)—Putting a new convert into a leadership role would tempt him to pride. Elders, therefore, are to be drawn from the spiritually mature men of the congregation (see notes on 5:22).

fall into the same condemnation as the devil (v. 6)—Satan's condemnation was due to pride over his position. It resulted in his fall from honor and authority (Isa. 14:12–14; Ezek. 28:11–19). The same kind of fall and judgment could easily happen to a new and weak believer put in a position of spiritual leadership.

good testimony . . . outside (v. 7)—A leader in the church must have an unimpeachable reputation in the unbelieving community, even though people there may disagree with his moral and theological stands. How can he make a spiritual impact on those who do not respect him (see Matt. 5:48)?

reverent (v. 8)—serious in mind and character; not silly or flippant about important matters

not double-tongued (v. 8)—Deacons must not say one thing to some people and something else to others; their speech must not be hypocritical, but honest and consistent.

not given to much wine (v. 8)—not preoccupied with drink (see note on v. 3)

not greedy (v. 8)—Like elders (see note on v. 3), deacons must not abuse their office to make money. Such a qualification was especially important in the early church, where deacons routinely handled money, distributing it to those in need.

the mystery (v. 9)—See 1 Corinthians 2:7; Ephesians 3:4–5. Appearing frequently in Paul's writings (see Rom. 11:25; 16:25; Eph. 1:9; 3:9; 6:19; Col. 2:2), the word "mystery" describes truth previously hidden, but now revealed, including Christ's incarnation (v. 16), Christ's indwelling of believers (Col. 1:26–27), the unity of Jews and Gentiles in the church (Eph. 3:4–6), the gospel (Col. 4:3), lawlessness (2 Thess. 2:7), and the rapture of the church (1 Cor. 15:51–52).

36

10 *But let these also first be tested; then let them serve as deacons, being found blameless.*

11 *Likewise, their wives must be reverent, not slanderers, temperate, faithful in all things.*

12 *Let deacons be the husbands of one wife, ruling their children and their own houses well.*

13 *For those who have served well as deacons obtain for themselves a good standing and great boldness in the faith which is in Christ Jesus.*

14 *These things I write to you, though I hope to come to you shortly;*

15 *but if I am delayed, I write so that you may know how you ought to conduct yourself in the house of God, which is the church of the living God, the pillar and ground of the truth.*

first be tested (v. 10)—The present tense of this verb indicates an ongoing evaluation of deacons' character and service by the church.

their wives (v. 11)—The Greek word rendered "wives" can also be translated "women." Paul likely here refers not to deacons' wives but to the women who serve as deacons. The use of the word "likewise" as an introduction (see v. 8) suggests a third group in addition to elders and deacons. Also, since Paul gave no requirements for elders' wives, there is no reason to assume these would be qualifications for deacons' wives.

not slanderers (v. 11)—"Slanderers" is the plural form of *diabolos*—a title frequently given to Satan (Matt. 13:39; Luke 4:3, 5–6, 13; 8:12; 1 Pet. 5:8; 1 John 3:8; Rev. 2:10; 12:9, 12; 20:2, 10). The women who serve must not be gossips.

temperate (v. 11)—See the note on verse 2.

faithful in all things (v. 11)—Women servants in the church, like their male counterparts (see note on v. 2), must be absolutely trustworthy in all aspects of their lives and ministries.

the husbands of one wife (v. 12)—See the note on verse 2.

ruling . . . their own houses well (v. 12)—See the note on verse 4.

I hope to come to you shortly (vv. 14–15)—The Greek grammar suggests Paul's meaning is "These things I write, although I had hoped to come to you sooner." Delayed in Macedonia, Paul sent Timothy this letter.

how you ought to conduct yourself (v. 15)—The second half of this verse expresses the theme of this epistle—setting things right in the church.

house of God (v. 15)—This is better translated "household." Believers are members of God's household (Gal. 6:10; Eph. 2:19; Heb. 3:6; 1 Pet. 4:17) and must act accordingly. This is not a reference to any building, but to the people who make up the true church.

church of the living God (v. 15)—The church is God's possession (Eph. 1:14; Titus 2:14; 1 Pet. 2:9). The title "the living God" has a rich Old Testament heritage (Josh. 3:10; 1 Sam. 17:26, 36; 2 Kings 19:4, 16; Ps. 42:2; 84:2; Isa. 37:4, 17; Jer. 10:10; 23:26; Dan. 6:20, 26; Hos. 1:10).

pillar and ground (v. 15)—Paul's imagery may have referred to the magnificent temple of Diana (Artemis) in Ephesus, which was supported by 127 gold-plated marble pillars. The word translated "ground" appears only here in the New Testament and denotes the foundation on which a building rests. The church upholds the truth of God's revealed Word.

the truth (v. 15)—the content of the Christian faith recorded in Scripture and summed up in verse 16

God . . . glory (v. 16)—This verse contains part of an early church hymn, as its uniformity, rhythm, and parallelism indicate. Its six lines form a concise summary of the truth of the gospel.

16 And without controversy great is the mystery of godliness: God was manifested in the flesh, justified in the Spirit, seen by angels, preached among the Gentiles, believed on in the world, received up in glory.

mystery of godliness (v. 16)—"Mystery" is that term used by Paul to indicate truth hidden in the Old Testament age and revealed in the New Testament (see note on v. 9). "Godliness" refers to the truths of salvation and righteousness in Christ, which produce holiness in believers; namely, the manifestation of true and perfect righteousness in Jesus Christ.

God was manifested (v. 16)—The better manuscripts read "He who" instead of "God." In either case, the reference is clearly to Christ, who manifested the invisible God to mankind (John 1:1–4; 14:9; Col. 1:15; Heb. 1:3; 2 Pet. 1:16–18).

in the flesh (v. 16)—This does not refer to sinful, fallen human nature here (see Rom. 7:18, 25; 8:8; Gal. 5:16–17), but merely humanness (see John 1:14; Rom. 1:3; 8:3; 9:5; 1 Pet. 3:18; 1 John 4:2–3).

justified in the Spirit (v. 16)—"Justified" means "righteous," so that "spirit" may be written with lower case "s," indicating a declaration of Christ's sinless spiritual righteousness (John 8:46; 2 Cor. 5:21; Heb. 4:15; 5:9; 7:26; 1 Pet. 2:21–22; 1 John 2:1), or it could refer to His vindication by the Holy Spirit (Rom. 1:4).

seen by angels (v. 16)—both by fallen (see Col. 2:15; 1 Pet. 3:18–20) and elect (Matt. 28:2; Luke 24:4–7; Acts 1:10–11; Heb. 1:6–9) angels

preached among the Gentiles (v. 16)—or, nations (see Matt. 24:14; 26:13; 28:19–20; Mark 13:10; Acts 1:8)

received up in glory (v. 16)—Christ's ascension and exaltation showed that the Father was pleased with Him and accepted His work fully (see Acts 1:9–10; Phil. 2:8–11; Heb. 1:3).

1) What qualities should be present in the lives of the bishops (elders) who lead the church?

_____

_____

_____

(Verses to consider: Phil. 3:17; 2 Tim. 2:15, 24; Titus 1:6–9)

2) Identify the actions or character flaws that can disqualify one from being a leader in the church.

_____

_____

_____

(Verses to consider: Matt. 6:24; 2 Tim. 2:24–25; Titus 1:7)

3) What is a deacon, and what is expected of one?

_____

_____

_____

_____

4) What requirements did Paul set for women serving in the church?

_____

_____

_____

_____

5) Why was Paul's instruction necessary?

_____

_____

_____

_____

GOING DEEPER

Writing to another church leader, Titus, Paul talked about how leaders were to be chosen. Read Titus 1:4–9.

4 *To Titus, a true son in our common faith: Grace, mercy, and peace from God the Father and the Lord Jesus Christ our Savior.*

5 *For this reason I left you in Crete, that you should set in order the things that are lacking, and appoint elders in every city as I commanded you—*

6 *if a man is blameless, the husband of one wife, having faithful children not accused of dissipation or insubordination.*

7 *For a bishop must be blameless, as a steward of God, not self-willed, not quick-tempered, not given to wine, not violent, not greedy for money,*

8 *but hospitable, a lover of what is good, sober-minded, just, holy, self-controlled,*

9 *holding fast the faithful word as he has been taught, that he may be able, by sound doctrine, both to exhort and convict those who contradict.*

Exploring the Meaning

6) Compare this list of qualifications with the one given Timothy. What is similar? What is different?

_____

_____

_____

_____

_____

7) Read 1 Peter 5:1–3. What added insights does this passage reveal about the right motives for those who lead God's church?

_____

_____

_____

_____

_____

(Verses to consider: 2 Cor. 4:1–7; 1 Thess. 1:5)

8) Read Mark 10:42–45. How did Jesus radically redefine leadership in His kingdom?

_____

_____

_____

_____

Truth for Today

The most important qualities leaders can demonstrate are not intelligence, a forceful personality, glibness, diligence, vision, administrative skills, decisiveness, courage, humor, tact, or any other similar natural attribute. Those all play a part, but the most desirable quality for any leader is integrity. While integrity is most desirable in secular leadership, its absence is fatal to spiritual leadership. Integrity is living what you teach and preach. That is why all the qualifications for leaders given in this passage describe their moral character. It is not the typical list a corporate analyst might come up with, because the issue is not leadership skills, but spiritual example. One who would lead people to Christlikeness must be a pattern of godly behavior for his people to follow. He must be above reproach in his moral life, home life, spiritual maturity, and public reputation.

REFLECTING ON THE TEXT

9) As you read through the list of leadership qualities found in chapter 3, which positive one(s) would you like to see more in your life? What negative traits do you need to put behind you?

_____

_____

_____

_____

10) Many church traditions recite the Apostles' Creed or the Nicene Creed. In 3:14–16, we find another statement of common belief (probably an early church hymn). If you were to summarize in a handful of statements what you believe, what would those statements be?

_____

_____

_____

_____

_____

11) What truths in Paul's "hymn" really stand out to you? Use these words as a model to write out your own hymn of praise to the Lord.

_____

_____

_____

_____

_____

PERSONAL RESPONSE

Write out additional reflections, questions you may have, or a prayer.

_____

_____

_____

_____

_____

_____

_____

_____

_____

_____

_____

_____

_____

_____

_____

_____

_____

_____

_____

_____

_____

_____

_____

_____

5

FALSE TEACHING VERSUS TRUTH

DRAWING NEAR

What kind of acceptance and tolerance do you think the Bible advocates?

_____

_____

_____

How does this compare or contrast with the brand of "tolerance" championed by our culture?

_____

_____

_____

When, if ever, do you think it is appropriate to confront another person about a false teaching they are following?

_____

_____

_____

_____

THE CONTEXT

Since the beginning of time, the earth has been at the center of the cosmic war between God and Satan. God reveals Himself through His Word and calls on people to respond. Satan attempts to blind human beings to the truth of God. The result is that many people believe satanic perversions to be the truth.

Ephesus was clearly inundated with false teachers. In chapters 2–3, the apostle Paul addressed some of the problems caused by these purveyors of spiritual error. He restated God's standards for leadership in the church and ended chapter 3 with a hymn affirming the essential truth of Christianity: the person and work of Jesus Christ. Now Paul deals directly with the false teachers themselves, focusing on their origin and content. He asserts that any tolerance of error is dishonoring to the God of truth. No deviations are to be allowed, and anyone who champions ungodly ideas is to be publicly rebuked.

KEYS TO THE TEXT

Godliness: This is a key word throughout the entire letter (3:16; 4:7–8; 6:3, 5–6, 11), indicating the need for the church to be called back to their pattern of holy living, which had been negatively affected by false doctrine. Godliness refers to having the proper attitude and response to God. It refers to the truths of salvation and righteousness in Christ, which produce holiness in believers—a manifestation of true and perfect righteousness in Jesus Christ.

Doctrine: A body of beliefs about God, humankind, Christ, the church, and other related concepts that are considered authoritative and thus worthy of acceptance by all members of the community of faith. Christ condemned the doctrine of the Pharisees because it was of human origin (Matt. 15:9; Mark 7:7). After Pentecost, Christian doctrine began to be systematized (Acts 2:42). The earliest doctrine of the Christian church declared: (1) that Jesus was the Messiah, the Christ; (2) that God had raised Him from the dead; and (3) that salvation was by faith in His name. These three truths were presented as a clear fulfillment of the promises of the Old Testament. Paul taught that true doctrine is essential for Christian growth (Eph. 4:11–16; 1 Tim. 4:6; 6:3; Titus 1:9) and that false doctrine destroys the church (Eph. 4:14; 2 Tim. 4:3). (*Nelson's New Illustrated Bible Dictionary*)

UNLEASHING THE TEXT

Read 4:1–16, noting the key words and definitions next to the passage.

1 Timothy 4:1–16 (NKJV)

the Spirit expressly says (v. 1)—Paul repeats to Timothy the warning he had given many years earlier to the Ephesian elders (Acts 20:29–30). The Holy Spirit through the Scriptures has repeatedly warned of the danger of apostasy (see Matt. 24:4–12; Acts 20:29–30; 2 Thess. 2:3–12; Heb. 3:12; 5:11–6:8; 10:26–31; 2 Pet. 3:3; 1 John 2:18; Jude 18).

in latter times. (v. 1)—The period from the first coming of Christ until His return (Acts 2:16–17; Heb. 1:1–2; 9:26; 1 Pet. 1:20; 1 John 2:18). Apostasy will exist throughout that period, reaching a climax shortly before Christ returns (see Matt. 24:12).

1   *Now the Spirit expressly says that in latter times some will depart from the faith, giving heed to deceiving spirits and doctrines of demons,*

2 *speaking lies in hypocrisy, having their own conscience seared with a hot iron,*

3 *forbidding to marry, and commanding to abstain from foods which God created to be received with thanksgiving by those who believe and know the truth.*

4 *For every creature of God is good, and nothing is to be refused if it is received with thanksgiving;*

5 *for it is sanctified by the word of God and prayer.*

6 *If you instruct the brethren in these things, you will be a good minister of Jesus Christ, nourished in the words of faith and of the good doctrine which you have carefully followed.*

depart from the faith (v. 1)—Those who fall prey to the false teachers will abandon the Christian faith. The Greek word for "depart" is the source of the English word "apostatize" and refers to someone moving away from an original position. These are professing or nominal Christians who associate with those who truly believe the gospel, but defect after believing lies and deception, thus revealing their true nature as unconverted (see 1 John 2:19).

deceiving spirits (v. 1)—This refers to those demonic spirits, either directly or through false teachers, who have wandered away from the truth and lead others to do the same. The most defining word to describe the entire operation of Satan and his demons is "deception" (see John 8:44).

doctrines of demons (v. 1)—This is not teaching about demons, but false teaching that originates from them. To sit under such teaching is to hear lies from the demonic realm (Eph. 6:12; James 3:15). The influence of demons will reach its peak during the Tribulation (2 Thess. 2:9; Rev. 9:2–11; 16:14; 20:2–3, 8, 10). Satan and demons constantly work the deceptions that corrupt and pervert God's Word.

speaking lies in hypocrisy (v. 2)—Literally "hypocritical lie-speakers," this refers to the human false teachers who propagate demon doctrine (see 1 John 4:1).

seared (v. 2)—This is a medical term referring to cauterization. False teachers can teach their hypocritical lies because their consciences have been desensitized (see Eph. 4:19), as if all the nerves that make them feel had been destroyed and turned into scar tissue by the burning of demonic deception.

forbidding to marry, and commanding to abstain from foods (v. 3)—This is a sample of the false teaching at Ephesus. Typically, it contained elements of truth, since Scripture commends both singleness (1 Cor. 7:25–35) and fasting (Matt. 6:16–17; 9:14–15). The deception came in making such human works a prerequisite for salvation—a distinguishing mark of all false religion. This ascetic teaching was probably influenced both by the Jewish sect known as the Essenes and contemporary Greek thought (which viewed matter as evil and spirit as good). Paul addressed this asceticism in Colossians 2:21–23. Neither celibacy nor any form of diet saves or sanctifies.

every creature of God is good (v. 4)—The false teachers' asceticism contradicted Scripture, which teaches that since God created both marriage and food (Gen. 1:28–31; 2:18–24; 9:3), they are intrinsically good (Gen. 1:31) and to be enjoyed with gratitude by believers. Obviously food and marriage are essential for life and procreation.

sanctified (v. 5)—This means to be set apart or dedicated to God for holy use. The means for accomplishing this are through thankful prayer and an understanding that the Word of God has set aside the temporary Mosaic dietary restrictions (Mark 7:19; Acts 10:9–15; Rom. 14:1–12; Col. 2:16–17). Contrast the unbeliever whose inner corruption and evil motives corrupt every good thing (Titus 1:15).

nourished . . . words of faith . . . good doctrine (v. 6)—Continual feeding on the truths of Scripture is essential to the spiritual health of all Christians (2 Tim. 3:16–17), but especially of spiritual leaders like Timothy. Only by reading the Word, studying it, meditating on it, and mastering its contents can a pastor fulfill his mandate (2 Tim. 2:15). Timothy had been doing so since childhood (2 Tim. 3:15), and Paul urged him to continue (see v. 16; 2 Tim. 3:14). "Words of faith" is a general reference to Scripture, God's revealed truth. "Good doctrine" indicates the theology Scripture teaches.

reject profane and old wives' fables (v. 7)—In addition to being committed to God's Word (see note on v. 6), believers must avoid all false teaching. Paul denounced such error as "profane" (worldly; the opposite of what is holy) "fables" (*mythos*, from which the English word *myths* derives), fit only for "old wives" (a common epithet denoting something fit only for the uneducated and philosophically unsophisticated).

exercise yourself (v. 7)—"Exercise" is an athletic term denoting the rigorous, self-sacrificing training an athlete undergoes.

7 But reject profane and old wives' fables, and exercise yourself toward godliness.

8 For bodily exercise profits a little, but godliness is profitable for all things, having promise of the life that now is and of that which is to come.

9 This is a faithful saying and worthy of all acceptance.

10 For to this end we both labor and suffer reproach, because we trust in the living God, who is the Savior of all men, especially of those who believe.

11 These things command and teach.

12 Let no one despise your youth, but be an example to the believers in word, in conduct, in love, in spirit, in faith, in purity.

profits a little (v. 8)—Bodily exercise is limited both in extent and duration; it affects only the physical body during this earthly life.

profitable for all things (v. 8)—in time and eternity

trust (v. 10)—This could also be "hope." Believers are saved in hope (see Rom. 8:24), and live and serve in light of that hope of eternal life (Titus 1:2; 3:7; see also Rom. 5:2). Working to the point of exhaustion and suffering rejection and persecution are acceptable because believers understand they are doing God's work—which is the work of salvation. That makes it worth all of the sacrifices (Phil. 1:12–18, 27–30; 2:17; Col. 1:24–25; 2 Tim. 1:6–12; 2:3–4, 9–10; 4:5–8).

the Savior of all men, especially of those who believe (v. 10)—Paul is obviously not teaching universalism, that all people will be saved in the spiritual and eternal sense, since the rest of Scripture clearly teaches that God will not save everyone. In fact, most adults will reject Him and spend eternity in hell (Matt. 25:41, 46; Rev. 20:11–15). Yet, the Greek word translated "especially" must mean that all men enjoy God's salvation in some way like those who believe enjoy His salvation. The simple explanation is that God is the Savior of all men, in a temporal sense, while He is the Savior of believers in an eternal sense. Paul's point is that while God graciously delivers believers from sin's condemnation and penalty because He was their substitute (2 Cor. 5:21), all men experience some earthly benefits from the goodness of God. Those benefits are (1) common grace—a term that describes God's goodness shown to all mankind universally (Ps. 145:9) in restraining sin (Rom. 2:15) and judgment (Rom. 2:3–6), maintaining order in society through government (Rom. 13:1–5), enabling man to appreciate beauty and goodness (Ps. 50:2), and showering him with temporal blessings (Matt. 5:45; Acts 14:15–17; 17:25); (2) compassion—the broken-hearted love of pity God shows to undeserving, unregenerate sinners (Exod. 34:6–7; Ps. 86:5; Dan. 9:9; Matt. 23:37; Luke 19:41–44; see Isa. 16:11–13; Jer. 48:35–37); (3) admonition to repent—God constantly warns sinners of their fate, demonstrating the heart of a compassionate Creator who has no pleasure in the death of the wicked (Ezek. 18:30–32; 33:11); and (4) the gospel invitation—salvation in Christ is indiscriminately offered to all (Matt. 11:28–29; 22:2–14; John 6:35–40; Rev. 22:17; see also John 5:39–40). God is, by nature, a saving God. That is, He finds no pleasure in the death of sinners. His saving character is revealed even in how He deals with those who will never believe, but only in those four temporal ways. See the notes on 2:6.

Let no one despise your youth (v. 12)—Greek culture placed great value on age and experience. Since Timothy was in his thirties, still young by the standards of that culture, he would have to earn respect by being a godly example. Because he had been with Paul since a young teenager, Timothy had much experience to mature him, so that looking down on him because he was under forty was inexcusable.

13 *Till I come, give attention to reading, to exhortation, to doctrine.*

14 *Do not neglect the gift that is in you, which was given to you by prophecy with the laying on of the hands of the eldership.*

15 *Meditate on these things; give yourself entirely to them, that your progress may be evident to all.*

16 *Take heed to yourself and to the doctrine. Continue in them, for in doing this you will save both yourself and those who hear you.*

be an example . . . in purity (v. 12)—Paul lists five areas (the better Greek manuscripts omit "in spirit") in which Timothy was to be an example to the church: "word" (speech; see Matt. 12:34–37; Eph. 4:25, 29, 31); "conduct" (righteous living; see Titus 2:10; 1 Pet. 1:15; 2:12; 3:16); "love" (self-sacrificial service for others; see John 15:13); "faith" (not belief, but faithfulness or commitment; see 1 Cor. 4:2); "purity" (especially sexual purity; see 3:2). Timothy's exemplary life in those areas would offset the disadvantage of his youth.

Till I come (v. 13)—See the note on 3:14.

give attention . . . to doctrine (v. 13)—These things were to be Timothy's constant practice; his way of life. "Reading" refers to the custom of public reading of Scripture in the church's worship service, followed by the exposition of the passage that had been read (see Neh. 8:1–8; Luke 4:16–27). "Exhortation" challenges those who hear the Word to apply it in their daily lives. It may involve rebuke, warning, encouragement, or comfort. "Doctrine" (teaching) refers to systematic instruction from the Word of God (see 3:2; Titus 1:9).

the gift (v. 14)—This refers to that grace given to Timothy and to all believers at salvation, which consisted of a God-designed, Spirit-empowered spiritual ability for the use of ministry (see Rom. 12:4–8; 1 Cor. 12:4–12; 1 Pet. 4:10–11). Timothy's gift (see 2 Tim. 1:6) was leadership with special emphasis on preaching (2 Tim. 4:2) and teaching (vv. 6, 11, 13; 6:2).

by prophecy (v. 14)—Timothy's gift was identified by a revelation from God (see note on 1:18) and apostolic confirmation (2 Tim. 1:6), probably when he joined Paul on the apostle's second missionary journey (Acts 16:1–3).

laying on of the hands of the eldership (v. 14)—See the note on 5:22. This public affirmation of Timothy's call to the ministry likely took place at the same time as the prophecy (see 2 Tim. 1:6). His call to the ministry was thus confirmed subjectively (by means of his spiritual gift), objectively (through the prophecy made about him), and collectively (by the affirmation of apostles and the church, represented by the elders).

progress (v. 15)—The word was used in military terms of an advancing force and in general terms of advancement in learning, understanding, or knowledge. Paul exhorted Timothy to let his progress toward Christlikeness be evident to all.

to yourself and to the doctrine (v. 16)—The priorities of a godly leader are summed up in his personal holiness and public teaching. All of Paul's exhortations in verses 6–16 fit into one or the other of those two categories.

you will save . . . yourself (v. 16)—Perseverance in believing the truth always accompanies genuine conversion (see Matt. 24:13; John 8:31; Rom. 2:7; Phil. 2:12–13; Col. 1:23).

those who hear you (v. 16)—By careful attention to his own godly life and faithful preaching of the Word, Timothy would continue to be the human instrument God used to bring the gospel and to save some who heard him. Though salvation is God's work, it is His pleasure to do it through human instruments.

1) What do Paul's harsh words about the purveyors of false teaching tell you about the importance of truth (vv. 1–5)?

_____

_____

_____

_____

(Verses to consider: Matt. 24:4–12; Acts 20:2–30; Col. 2:16–23)

2) Describe the personal character qualities of an excellent minister spotlighted by Paul in 4:6–11.

_____

_____

_____

_____

3) What ministry standards of excellence are expected of church leaders (4:12–16)?

_____

_____

_____

_____

(Verses to consider: 1 Pet. 4:10–11)

4) Note the advice Paul gives to Timothy in verses 12–14. What does it mean to be an "example" of these things?

_____

_____

_____

_____

Going Deeper

Paul never taught what he himself did not do. Read about his faithful leadership in 1 Thessalonians 2:7–12.

7 But we were gentle among you, just as a nursing mother cherishes her own children.

8 So, affectionately longing for you, we were well pleased to impart to you not only the gospel of God, but also our own lives, because you had become dear to us.

9 For you remember, brethren, our labor and toil; for laboring night and day, that we might not be a burden to any of you, we preached to you the gospel of God.

10 You are witnesses, and God also, how devoutly and justly and blamelessly we behaved ourselves among you who believe;

11 as you know how we exhorted, and comforted, and charged every one of you, as a father does his own children,

12 that you would walk worthy of God who calls you into His own kingdom and glory.

Exploring the Meaning

5) How did Paul model the spiritual virtues of love and servanthood when ministering to the Thessalonians?

_____

_____

_____

_____

_____

6) For what purpose did Paul exhort and encourage these churches? What was his ultimate goal for them?

_____

_____

_____

_____

_____

7) Read 2 Peter 2:1 and Revelation 12:9. What role does the enemy play in propagating false doctrine? What end awaits both Satan and false teachers?

_____

_____

_____

_____

8) Read 1 Corinthians 9:24–27. In what ways is spiritual self-discipline the path to godly living?

_____

_____

_____

_____

(Verses to consider Matt. 25:21; 2 Cor. 7:1; 2 Tim. 2:3–5)

Truth for Today

The single greatest tool of leadership is the power of an exemplary life. The Puritan writer Thomas Brooks said, "Example is the most powerful rhetoric." Setting an example of godly living that others can follow is the *sine qua non* of excellence in ministry. When a manifest pattern of godliness is missing, the power is drained out of preaching, leaving it a hollow, empty shell. A minister's life is his most powerful message, and must reinforce what he says or he may as well not say it. Authoritative preaching is undermined if there is not a virtuous life backing it up.

Reflecting on the Text

9) Paul spoke to Timothy of the need to be "nourished in the words of faith" (v. 6). Describe your biblical diet. Are you being nourished regularly through the reading of the Scriptures, or are you malnourished? What needs to change?

_____

_____

_____

10) What spiritual disciplines do you need to practice this week in order to pursue godliness with more consistency?

_____

_____

_____

11) This passage speaks of being an example to other believers and living in such a way that your spiritual progress is obvious to all. Evaluate yourself in these regards. What kind of an example are you? How evident is your spiritual progress? What one change can you make that would make a real difference in your spiritual growth?

_____

_____

_____

_____

Personal Response

Write out additional reflections, questions you may have, or a prayer.

_____

_____

_____

_____

_____

_____

_____

_____

_____

_____

_____

_____

_____

_____

_____

_____

_____

_____

_____

_____

_____

_____

_____

_____

_____

_____

_____

_____

_____

_____

_____

_____

_____

_____

_____

_____

_____

6

PASTORAL RESPONSIBILITIES

DRAWING NEAR

When it comes to caring for the elderly and needy, who on the following list should bear the responsibility:

⟋ the government?

⟋ the extended family?

⟋ the church?

⟋ the individuals themselves?

Why do you think so?

_____

_____

_____

Think about different pastors or elders you have known. Who stands out in your mind as having served with exceptional commitment and excellence? What sets them apart? How have you personally benefited from their ministry?

_____

_____

_____

_____

THE CONTEXT

No amount of formal training can prepare a pastor for every contingency he will face in the Lord's work. This is true now and it was true in the first century. Thus, it is not surprising to find a passage like this one that contains a broad array of Spirit-inspired counsel for Timothy, the young leader of the Ephesian church.

In this passage Paul discusses several areas of church business. He gives the Scriptural mandate to respect the older men and women in the church, and to care for women who have lost their husbands. God's great concern for widows only reinforces this command (see Deut. 26:10–12; Ps. 68:5; James 1:27). Paul then explains how to restore proper pastoral oversight, and sets forth the church's obligations to honor, protect, rebuke, and select elders. He offers instructions for servants and masters, so perhaps the Ephesian believers were struggling to maintain a biblical work ethic in the world of slavery. One can only imagine the great delight Timothy must have felt when he first read this relevant and immensely practical bit of wise, heaven-sent counsel.

KEYS TO THE TEXT

Exhort: Literally "to call to one's side," this emphasizes a strong urging, directing, and insisting on following the principles for correct behavior in the workplace. This Greek word refers to coming alongside someone to help, and is related to a title for the Holy Spirit (see John 14:16, 26; 15:26; 16:7). It may best be translated "strengthen." We are to strengthen our fellow believers (see Gal. 6:1–2) in the same way the Scripture and the Holy Spirit do.

Bondservants: This can be translated "slaves." First-century slaves resembled the indentured servants of the American colonial period. In many cases, slaves were better off than day laborers, since much of their food, clothing, and shelter was provided. The system of slavery served as the economic structure in the Roman world, and the master-slave relationship closely parallels the modern employer-employee relationship. This term also refers to people who are in submission to another, and is often used in connection with Jesus serving the Father (Phil. 2:7), and believers serving God (1 Pet. 2:16; Rom. 1:1; Gal. 1:10; 2 Tim. 2:24; James 1:1) and other believers (Gal. 5:13).

UNLEASHING THE TEXT

Read 5:1–6:2, noting the key words and definitions next to the passage.

rebuke (v. 1)—Some translations add "sharply" to the word "rebuke," which fills out the intensity of the Greek term. An older sinning believer is to be shown respect by not being addressed with harsh words (see 2 Tim. 2:24–25).

1 Timothy 5:1–6:2 (NKJV)

1 *Do not rebuke an older man, but exhort him as a father, younger men as brothers,*

2 *older women as mothers, younger women as sisters, with all purity.*

an older man (v. 1)—in this context, the Greek is indicating older men generally, not the office of elder. the younger Timothy was to confront sinning older men with deference and honor, which is clearly inferred from Old Testament principles (see Lev. 19:32; Job 32:4, 6; Prov. 4:1–4; 16:31; 20:29).

3 *Honor widows who are really widows.*

4 *But if any widow has children or grandchildren, let them first learn to show piety at home and to repay their parents; for this is good and acceptable before God.*

5 *Now she who is really a widow, and left alone, trusts in God and continues in supplications and prayers night and day.*

6 *But she who lives in pleasure is dead while she lives.*

7 *And these things command, that they may be blameless.*

8 *But if anyone does not provide for his own, and especially for those of his household, he has denied the faith and is worse than an unbeliever.*

9 *Do not let a widow under sixty years old be taken into the number, and not unless she has been the wife of one man,*

Honor (v. 3)—This means "to show respect or care," "to support," or "to treat graciously." Although it includes meeting all kinds of needs, Paul had in mind here not only this broad definition but primarily financial support (see Exod. 20:12; Matt. 15:1–6; 27:9).

really widows (v. 3)—Not all widows are truly alone and without resources. Financial support from the church is mandatory only for widows who have no means to provide for their daily needs.

widow has children or grandchildren (v. 4)—Families, not the church, have the first responsibility for their own widows.

repay their parents (v. 4)—Children and grandchildren are indebted to those who brought them into the world, reared them, and loved them. Fulfilling this responsibility is a mark of godly obedience (see Exod. 20:12).

left alone (v. 5)—See the note on verse 3. The form of this Greek word denotes a permanent condition of being forsaken and left without resources. She is "really" a widow, since there is no family to support her.

trusts in God (v. 5)—a continual state or settled attitude of hope in God (see 1 Kings 17:8–16; Jer. 49:11). Since she has no one else, she pleads with God as her only hope.

dead while she lives (v. 6)— a widow who lives a worldly, immoral, ungodly life may be alive physically, but her lifestyle proves she is unregenerate and spiritually dead (see Eph. 2:1).

blameless (v. 7)—Means "above reproach," so that no one can fault their conduct.

if (v. 8)—This would be better translated "since." Paul negatively restated the positive principle of verse 4, using the Greek construction that implies the condition is true, suggesting that there were numerous violations of that principle at Ephesus. Any believer who fails to obey this command is guilty of (1) denying the principle of compassionate Christian love (see John 13:35; Rom. 5:5; 1 Thess. 4:9); and (2) being "worse than an unbeliever." Most pagans naturally fulfill this duty, so believers who have God's command and power to carry it out and do not, behave worse than pagans (see 1 Cor. 5:1–2.).

under sixty (v. 9)—In New Testament culture, sixty was considered retirement age. By that age, older women would have completed their child-rearing and would have the time, maturity, and character to devote their lives in service to God and the church. They also would not be likely to remarry and become preoccupied with that commitment.

be taken into the number (v. 9)—More clearly rendered, "be put on the list." This was not a list of those widows eligible for specially recognized church support (all widows in the church who had no other means of support were; v. 3), but rather those eligible for specially recognized church ministry (see Titus 2:3–5).

the wife of one man (v. 9)—Literally "one-man woman" (see 3:2, 12). It does not exclude women who have been married more than once (see v. 14; 1 Cor. 7:39), but it refers to a woman totally devoted and faithful to her husband, a wife who had displayed purity of thought and action in her marriage.

55

has brought up children (v. 10)—This views the godly widow as a Christian mother who has nourished or reared children that have followed the Lord (see note on 2:15).

washed the saints' feet (v. 10)—This refers to the menial duty of slaves. It is used literally and metaphorically of widows who have humble servants' hearts (see John 13:5–17).

every good work (v. 10)—See Dorcas in Acts 9:36–39.

to grow wanton (v. 11)—This would be better translated "to feel the impulses of sensual desires"—an expression that includes all that is involved in the marriage relationship, including sexual passion. Paul saw the danger that younger widows might want to escape from their vows to remain single (see note on v. 12) and be devoted only to God's service (see Num. 30:9); he knew the negative impact such feelings could have on young widows' personal lives and ministry within the church. Such women were also marked out by false teachers as easy prey (2 Tim. 3:6–7), causing them to leave the truth (v. 15).

10 well reported for good works: if she has brought up children, if she has lodged strangers, if she has washed the saints' feet, if she has relieved the afflicted, if she has diligently followed every good work.

11 But refuse the younger widows; for when they have begun to grow wanton against Christ, they desire to marry,

12 having condemnation because they have cast off their first faith.

13 And besides they learn to be idle, wandering about from house to house, and not only idle but also gossips and busybodies, saying things which they ought not.

14 Therefore I desire that the younger widows marry, bear children, manage the house, give no opportunity to the adversary to speak reproachfully.

15 For some have already turned aside after Satan.

16 If any believing man or woman has widows, let them relieve them, and do not let the church be burdened, that it may relieve those who are really widows.

cast off their first faith (v. 12)—in classical Greek, "faith" could also mean "pledge." Taken that way here, it refers to a specific covenant young widows made when asking to be included on the widows' list. Likely, they promised to devote the rest of their lives in service to the church and the Lord. Though well-meaning at the time of their need and bereavement, they were surely to desire marriage again (see v. 11), and thus renege on their original pledge.

gossips (v. 13)—Such people speak nonsense, talk idly, make empty charges, or even accuse others with malicious words. This idleness and talk also made them suitable targets for the false teachers (1:6).

busybodies (v. 13)—Literally "one who moves around," this implies that such people pry into things that do not concern them; they do not mind their own business.

bear children (v. 14)—The younger widows were still of childbearing age. Although they had lost their first husbands, there was still the potential privilege and blessing of remarrying and having children (see notes on 2:15; see Ps. 127:3, 5).

manage the house (v. 14)—The Greek term denotes all the aspects of household administration, not merely the rearing of children. The home is the domain where a married woman fulfills herself in God's design (see Titus 2:4–5).

Satan (v. 15)—the devil, the believer's adversary (see Job 1:6–12; 2:1–7; Isa. 14:12–15; Ezek. 28:12–15; Rev. 12:9)

woman (v. 16)—Paul restates the message of verses 4–8 with the addition that as the situation warrants, Christian women are included in this responsibility for support of widows.

17 Let the elders who rule well be counted worthy of double honor, especially those who labor in the word and doctrine.

18 For the Scripture says, "You shall not muzzle an ox while it treads out the grain," and, "The laborer is worthy of his wages."

19 Do not receive an accusation against an elder except from two or three witnesses.

20 Those who are sinning rebuke in the presence of all, that the rest also may fear.

21 I charge you before God and the Lord Jesus Christ and the elect angels that you observe these things without prejudice, doing nothing with partiality.

elders (v. 17)—This identifies the "bishop" (3:1) or overseer, who is also called pastor (Eph. 4:11) (see notes on 3:1–7; Titus 1:6–9).

rule well (v. 17)—Elders are spiritual rulers in the church (see 1 Thess. 5:12–13; Heb. 13:7, 17).

double honor (v. 17)—Elders who serve with greater commitment, excellence, and effort should have greater acknowledgment from their congregations. This expression does not mean such men should receive exactly twice as much remuneration as others, but because they have earned such respect, it should be paid to them more generously.

especially (v. 17)—This means "chiefly" or "particularly." Implicit is the idea that some elders will work harder than others and be more prominent in ministry.

labor (v. 17)—Literally "work to the point of fatigue or exhaustion," this Greek word stresses the effort behind the work more than the amount of work.

word and doctrine (v. 17)—This would be better translated "preaching and teaching" (see note on 4:13). The first emphasizes proclamation, along with exhortation and admonition, and calls for a heart response to the Lord. The second is an essential fortification against heresy and puts more stress on instruction.

for the Scripture says (v. 18)—a typical formula for introducing biblical references, in this instance both an Old Testament (Deut. 25:4) and New Testament (Luke 10:7) one. It is also very significant that this is a case of one New Testament writer (Paul) affirming the inspiration of another by referring to Luke's writing as "Scripture" (see 2 Pet. 3:15–16), which shows the high view that the early church took of New Testament Scripture.

two or three witnesses (v. 19)—Serious accusations against elders must be investigated and confirmed by the same process as established in Matthew 18:15–20. This process for the whole church also applies to elders. This demand does not place elders beyond successful accusation, but protects them from frivolous, evil accusers, by demanding the same process of confirmation of sin as for all in the church.

Those who are sinning (v. 20)—elders who continue in any kind of sin after the confrontation of two or three witnesses, especially any that violates the qualifications to serve (3:2–7)

in the presence of all (v. 20)—This refers to the other elders and the congregation. The third step of confrontation, established in Matthew 18:17, is to tell the church, so that they can all confront the person and call him to repentance.

charge . . . God . . . Lord (v. 21)—See 6:13; 2 Timothy 4:1.

the elect angels (v. 21)—This refers to "chosen angels," the unfallen angels, as opposed to Satan and his demons. This indicates that God's sovereign purpose to choose those beings who would be part of His eternal kingdom included angels whom He chose to eternal glory. Christians are also called "elect" (Rom. 8:33; 11:7; Col. 3:12; 2 Tim. 2:10; Titus 1:1; 1 Pet. 1:2; 2 John 1, 13).

without prejudice . . . partiality
(v. 21)—All discipline of elders is to be done fairly, without pre-judgment or personal prefer-ence, according to the standards of Scripture.

Do not lay hands on . . . hastily
(v. 22)—This refers to the cere-mony that affirmed a man's suit-ability for and acceptance into public ministry as an elder/pas-tor/overseer. This came from the Old Testament practice of lay-ing hands on a sacrificial animal to identify with it (Exod. 29:10, 15, 19; Lev. 4:15; see also Num. 8:10; 27:18–23; Deut. 34:9; Matt. 19:15; Acts 8:17–18; 9:17; Heb. 6:2). "Hastily" refers to proceed-ing with this ceremony without a thorough investigation and preparation period to be certain of the man's qualifications (as in 3:1–7).

22 Do not lay hands on anyone hastily, nor share in other people's sins; keep yourself pure.

23 No longer drink only water, but use a little wine for your stomach's sake and your frequent infirmities.

24 Some men's sins are clearly evident, preceding them to judgment, but those of some men follow later.

25 Likewise, the good works of some are clearly evident, and those that are otherwise cannot be hidden.

6:1 Let as many bondservants as are under the yoke count their own masters worthy of all honor, so that the name of God and His doctrine may not be blasphemed.

2 And those who have believing masters, let them not despise them because they are brethren, but rather serve them because those who are benefited are believers and beloved. Teach and exhort these things.

nor share in other people's sins (v. 22)—This refers to the sin of hasty ordination, which makes those responsible culpable for the man's sin of serving as an unqualified elder and, thus, misleading people.

keep yourself pure (v. 22)—Some versions translate "pure" as "free from sin." Paul wanted Timothy, by not participating in the recognition of unqualified elders, to remain untainted by others' sins. The church desperately needed qualified spiritual leaders, but the selection had to be carefully executed.

No longer drink only water (v. 23)—Water in the ancient world was often polluted and carried many diseases. Therefore Paul urged Timothy not to risk illness, not even for the sake of a commitment to abstinence from wine. Apparently Timothy avoided wine so as not to place himself in harm's way (see note on 3:3).

use a little wine . . . infirmities (v. 23)—Paul wanted Timothy to use wine which, because of fermenta-tion, acted as a disinfectant to protect his health from the harmful effects of impure water. With this advice, however, Paul was not advocating that Timothy lower the high standard of behavior for leaders (see Num. 6:1–4; Prov. 31:4–5).

sins are clearly evident (v. 24)—The sins of some men are manifest for all to see, thus disqualifying them out of hand for service as elders.

preceding them to judgment (v. 24)—The known sins of the unqualified announce those men's guilt and unfitness before all. "Judgment" refers to the church's process for determining men's suitability to serve as elders.

follow later (v. 24)—The sins of other candidates for elder will come to light in time, perhaps even during the scrutiny of the evaluation process.

under the yoke (v. 1)—a colloquial expression describing submissive service under another's authority, not necessarily describing an abusive relationship (see Matt. 11:28–30)

masters (v. 1)—The Greek word for "master," while giving us the English word "despot," does not carry a negative connotation. Instead, it refers to one with absolute and unrestricted authority.

all honor (v. 1)—This translates into diligent and faithful labor for one's employer (see Eph. 6:5–9; Col. 3:22–25).

58

His doctrine (v. 1)—This is the revelation of God summed up in the gospel. How believers act while under the authority of another affects how people view the message of salvation Christians proclaim (see Titus 2:5-14). Displaying a proper attitude of submission and respect, and performing quality work, help make the gospel message believable (Matt. 5:48).

believing masters (v. 2)—The tendency might be to assume one's equality in Christ with a Christian master and disdain the authority related to work roles. On the contrary, working for a Christian should produce more loyal and diligent service out of love for the brethren.

1) What counsel does Paul give for dealing with sin in the spiritual family (5:1-2, 19-20)?

2) How were widows to be cared for (5:3-16)? What distinctions were made, and why?

(Verses to consider: Exod. 22:22-24; Deut. 26:10-12; James 1:27)

3) Put in your own words the gist of Paul's instruction about biblical eldership (5:17-25).

(Verses to consider: Acts 20:28; 1 Thess. 5:12, 13; Heb. 13:7, 17)

4) What principles did Paul give regarding acceptable behavior for Christian employees (6:1–2)?

_____

_____

_____

_____

_____

(Verses to consider: 1 Cor. 10:31; Eph. 6:5–8; Col. 3:22–25; Titus 2:9–10)

GOING DEEPER

For more of Paul's teaching about employee/employer relationships, read Ephesians 6:5–9.

5 *Bondservants, be obedient to those who are your masters according to the flesh, with fear and trembling, in sincerity of heart, as to Christ;*

6 *not with eyeservice, as men-pleasers, but as bondservants of Christ, doing the will of God from the heart,*

7 *with goodwill doing service, as to the Lord, and not to men,*

8 *knowing that whatever good anyone does, he will receive the same from the Lord, whether he is a slave or free.*

9 *And you, masters, do the same things to them, giving up threatening, knowing that your own Master also is in heaven, and there is no partiality with Him.*

EXPLORING THE MEANING

5) What attitudes should Christian employers and employees have? Why do you think Paul gave these specific instructions?

_____

_____

_____

_____

_____

6) Read Luke 7:11–17 for an encounter that Jesus had with a needy widow. What makes the raising of this young man especially poignant? What do we learn about the heart of God from this miracle?

_____

_____

_____

_____

_____

_____

7) Read 1 Corinthians 9:1–14. What does Paul say here about elders being entitled to financial support?

_____

_____

_____

_____

_____

_____

_____

(Verses to consider: Luke 10:7; Phil. 4:10–20)

TRUTH FOR TODAY

For the believer, work is a sacred duty. A Christian sees everything he does in reference to his relationship with God. The Reformers stressed that point. There is no aspect of life or conduct, however apparently insignificant, which should not be directed to the glory of God. Every legitimate job has intrinsic value because it is the arena in which believers live out their Christian lives. Christianity is not a hothouse religion, but one that survives and triumphs in the real world. Believers most commonly interact with that world in the work place, as they live out their faith on their jobs. They are to be a "city that is set on a hill" (Matt. 5:14). Christians must be concerned that their conduct on the job shows others the power of Jesus Christ to transform a life. Believers' work performance will bring either praise or blasphemy to the name of God.

REFLECTING ON THE TEXT

8) Think about a practical and specific way in which you can be a more excellent employee this week. Write down your ideas.

_____

_____

_____

9) Do you have any close Christian friends who are engaged in sinful or questionable behaviors? What is God leading you to do—exhort them gently, pray for them, other?

_____

_____

_____

10) What widows in your church can you encourage and help this week? List some specific ways you could offer assistance.

_____

_____

_____

_____

PERSONAL RESPONSE

Write out additional reflections, questions you may have, or a prayer.

_____

_____

_____

_____

_____

~7~
THE MAN OF GOD

1 Timothy 6:3–21

DRAWING NEAR

In this study, Paul warns Timothy about the dangers of greed. What material possessions do you worry most about losing? Why?

_____

_____

_____

_____

If you can, describe a time in your life when you truly experienced contentment. Explain the circumstances.

_____

_____

_____

_____

THE CONTEXT

As this letter comes to a close, Paul wraps up his instructions to Timothy by giving some further identifying markers for false and corrupt teachers in the church. He counsels the young pastor what to teach those who are rich in material possessions, those who have more than the mere essentials of food, clothing, and shelter. Paul does not condemn such people, nor command them to get rid of their wealth. He does call them to be good stewards of their God-given resources.

He fervently urges his protégé to resist all these temptations and to cling to his divine calling. Timothy was the "man of God" for the church at Ephesus. His effectiveness would depend upon what he fought for and what he fled from.

KEYS TO THE TEXT

Contentment: This Greek word means "self-sufficiency"; stoic philosophers used it to describe a person who was unflappable and unmoved by external circumstances. Christians ought to be satisfied and sufficient, for God Himself is the source of true contentment. They should have no need to seek for more than what God has already supplied in and through Himself.

Man of God: A term used in the New Testament only for Timothy (see 2 Tim. 3:17). As a technical term it is used about seventy times in the Old Testament, always to refer to a man who officially spoke for God (see Deut. 33:1). This indicates that the letter is primarily directed to Timothy, exhorting him to be faithful and strong in light of persecution and difficulty—particularly with Paul's death drawing near. The man of God is known by what he flees from (v. 11), follows after (v. 11), fights for (v. 12), and is faithful to (vv. 13–14). The key to his success in all these endeavors can be found in the perfection produced in him by the Scriptures (2 Tim. 3:16–17).

UNLEASHING THE TEXT

Read 6:3–21, noting the key words and definitions next to the passage.

1 Timothy 6:3–21 (NKJV)

If anyone teaches . . . (vv. 3–5)—Paul identifies three characteristics of false teachers: (1) they "teach otherwise"—a different doctrine, or any teaching that contradicts God's revelation in Scripture; (2) they do "not consent to wholesome words"—they do not agree with sound, healthy teaching, specifically the teaching contained in Scripture; and (3) they reject "doctrine which accords with godliness"—teaching not based on Scripture will always result in an unholy life.

3 *If anyone teaches otherwise and does not consent to wholesome words, even the words of our Lord Jesus Christ, and to the doctrine which accords with godliness,*

4 *he is proud, knowing nothing, but is obsessed with disputes and arguments over words, from which come envy, strife, reviling, evil suspicions,*

5 *useless wranglings of men of corrupt minds and destitute of the truth, who suppose that godliness is a means of gain. From such withdraw yourself.*

Instead of godliness, false teachers will be marked by sin.

disputes and arguments over words (v. 4)—"Disputes" refers to idle speculation; "arguments over words" literally means "word battles." Because proud, ignorant false teachers do not understand divine truth (2 Cor. 2:14), they obsess over terminology and attack the reliability and authority of Scripture. Every kind of strife is mentioned to indicate that false teachers produce nothing of benefit out of their fleshly, corrupt, and empty minds (v. 5).

destitute of the truth (v. 5)—These false teachers are in a state of apostasy; that is, although they once knew and seemed to embrace the truth, they turned to openly reject it. The Greek word for "destitute" means "to steal," "to rob," or "to deprive", and its form here indicates that someone or something was pulled away from contact with the truth (it does not mean they were ever saved).

a means of gain (v. 5)—Almost always behind all the efforts of the hypocritical, lying (4:2), false teachers is the driving motivation of monetary gain.

6 Now godliness with contentment is great gain.

7 For we brought nothing into this world, and it is certain we can carry nothing out.

8 And having food and clothing, with these we shall be content.

9 But those who desire to be rich fall into temptation and a snare, and into many foolish and harmful lusts which drown men in destruction and perdition.

10 For the love of money is a root of all kinds of evil, for which some have strayed from the faith in their greediness, and pierced themselves through with many sorrows.

11 But you, O man of God, flee these things and pursue righteousness, godliness, faith, love, patience, gentleness.

12 Fight the good fight of faith, lay hold on eternal life, to which you were also called and have confessed

From such withdraw yourself. (v. 5)—This phrase does not appear in the better manuscripts, although the idea expressed is self-evident.

having food and clothing . . . be content (v. 8)—the basic necessities of life are what ought to make Christians content. Paul does not condemn having possessions, as long as God graciously provides them (v. 17). He does, however, condemn a self-indulgent desire for money, which results from discontentment (see Matt. 6:33).

desire to be rich fall into temptation (v. 9)—"Desire" refers to a settled wish born of reason and clearly describes those guilty of greed. The form of the Greek verb for "fall" indicates that those who have such a desire are continually falling into temptation. Greedy people are compulsive—they are continually trapped in sins by their consuming desire to acquire more.

destruction and perdition (v. 9)—Such greed may lead these people to suffer the tragic end of destruction and hell. These terms refer to the eternal punishment of the wicked.

love of money (v. 10)—This is literally "affection for silver." in the context, this sin applies to false teachers specifically, but the principle is true universally. Money itself is not evil since it is a gift from God (Deut. 8:18); Paul condemns only the love of it (see Matt. 6:24), which is so characteristic of false teachers (see 1 Pet. 5:2; 2 Pet. 2:1–3, 15).

strayed from the faith (v. 10)—This means they have strayed from the body of Christian truth. Gold has replaced God for these apostates, who have turned away from pursuing the things of God in favor of money.

these things (v. 11)—love of money and all that goes with it (vv. 6–10), along with the other proud obsessions of false teachers (vv. 3–5)

righteousness, godliness (v. 11)—"Righteousness" means to do what is right, in relation to both God and man, and it emphasizes outward behavior. "Godliness" (see note on 2:2) refers to one's reverence for God and could be translated "God-likeness."

Fight the good fight of faith (v. 12)—The Greek word for "fight" gives us the English word *agonize*, and was used in both military and athletic endeavors to describe the concentration, discipline, and extreme effort needed to win. The "good fight of faith" is the spiritual conflict with Satan's kingdom of darkness in which all men of God are necessarily involved.

lay hold on eternal life (v. 12)—Paul is here admonishing Timothy to "get a grip" on the reality of the matters associated with eternal life, so that he would live and minister with a heavenly and eternal perspective.

to which you were also called (v. 12)—refers to God's effectual, sovereign call of Timothy to salvation (see note on Rom. 1:7)

good confession (v. 12)—Timothy's public confession of faith in the Lord Jesus Christ, which likely occurred at his baptism and again when he was ordained to the ministry (4:14; 2 Tim. 1:6)

urge ... God ... Christ (v. 13)—See 5:21; see note on 2 Timothy 4:1.

the good confession before Pontius Pilate (v. 13)—Knowing that such a confession would cost Him His life, Jesus nevertheless confessed that He was truly the King and Messiah (John 18:33–37). He never evaded danger; He boldly and trustfully committed Himself to God who raises the dead.

this commandment (v. 14)—This refers to the entire revealed Word of God, which Paul

the good confession in the presence of many witnesses.

13 I urge you in the sight of God who gives life to all things, and before Christ Jesus who witnessed the good confession before Pontius Pilate,

14 that you keep this commandment without spot, blameless until our Lord Jesus Christ's appearing,

15 which He will manifest in His own time, He who is the blessed and only Potentate, the King of kings and Lord of lords,

16 who alone has immortality, dwelling in unapproachable light, whom no man has seen or can see, to whom be honor and everlasting power. Amen.

17 Command those who are rich in this present age not to be haughty, nor to trust in uncertain riches but

charged Timothy to preach (2 Tim. 4:2). Paul also repeatedly encouraged Timothy to guard it (v. 20; 1 Tim. 1:18–19; 4:6, 16; 2 Tim. 1:13–4; 2:15–18).

appearing (v. 14)—This refers to the Lord's return to earth in glory (see 2 Tim. 4:1–8; Titus 2:13) to judge and to establish His kingdom (Matt. 24:27, 29–30; 25:31). Christ's imminent return ought to motivate the man of God to remain faithful to his calling until he dies or the Lord returns (see Acts 1:8–11; 1 Cor. 4:5; Rev. 22:12).

in His own time (v. 15)—the time, known only to Him, that God established in eternity past for Christ to return

Potentate (v. 15)—This word comes from a Greek word group that basically means "power," but here it is best translated "sovereign." God is absolutely sovereign and omnipotently rules over everything everywhere.

King of kings and Lord of lords (v. 15)—a title used of Christ (Rev. 17:14; 19:16) is here used of God the Father. Paul probably used this title for God to confront the cult of emperor worship, intending to communicate that only God is sovereign and worthy of worship.

whom no man has seen or can see (v. 16)—God in spirit is invisible (see 1:17; Job 23:8–9; John 1:18; 5:37; Col. 1:15) and, therefore, unapproachable in the sense that sinful man has never seen nor can he ever see His full glory (see Exod. 33:20; Isa. 6:1–5).

haughty (v. 17)—This means "to have an exalted opinion of oneself." Those who have an abundance of worldly possessions are constantly tempted to look down on others and act superior. Riches and pride often go together, and the wealthier a person is, the more he is tempted to be proud (Prov. 18:23; 28:11; James 2:1–4).

uncertain riches ... gives us richly (v. 17)—Those who have much tend to trust in their wealth (see Prov. 23:4–5). But God provides far more security than any earthly investment can ever give (Eccl. 5:18–20; Matt. 6:19–21).

in the living God, who gives us richly all things to enjoy.

18 Let them do good, that they be rich in good works, ready to give, willing to share,

19 storing up for themselves a good foundation for the time to come, that they may lay hold on eternal life.

20 O Timothy! Guard what was committed to your trust, avoiding the profane and idle babblings and contradictions of what is falsely called knowledge—

21 by professing it some have strayed concerning the faith. Grace be with you. Amen.

ready to give (v. 18)—The Greek word means "liberal" or "bountiful." Those believers who have money must use it in meeting the needs of others, unselfishly and generously (see Acts 4:32–37; 2 Cor. 8:1–4).

storing up . . . a good foundation (v. 19)—"Storing up" can be translated "amassing a treasure," while "foundation" can refer to a fund. The idea is that the rich in this world should not be concerned with receiving a return on their earthly investment. Those who make eternal investments will be content to receive their dividends in heaven (see Luke 16:1–13).

lay hold on eternal life (v. 19)—See the note on verse 12.

what was committed to your trust (v. 20)—This translates one Greek word, which means "deposit." The deposit Timothy was to guard was the truth—the divine revelation that God committed to his care. Every Christian, especially if he is in ministry, has that sacred trust to guard the revelation of God (see 1 Cor. 4:1; 1 Thess. 2:3–4).

what is falsely called knowledge (v. 20)—This refers to false doctrine—anything claiming to be the truth that is in fact a lie. False teachers typically claim to have the superior knowledge (as in Gnosticism). They claim to know the transcendent secrets, but actually are ignorant and infantile in their understanding (see Col. 2:8).

Grace be with you. (v. 21)—Paul's closing salutation is plural, i.e., "you all"—it goes beyond Timothy to the entire congregation at Ephesus. All believers require the grace of God to preserve the truth and pass it on to the next generation.

1) What clues does Paul give Timothy for identifying false teachers (vv. 3–5)?

_____

_____

_____

(Verses to consider: Gal. 1:6–9; 2 Pet. 2:10–22; 3:14–16; Jude 4, 8–16)

2) In what ways is the love of money a snare (vv. 6–10)?

_____

_____

_____

(Verses to consider: Deut. 8:11–18; Prov. 11:24–25; Matt. 6:19–21, 24)

3) Circle all the commands that Paul gives Timothy in verses 11–14. Summarize the heart of Paul's exhortation to Timothy. Why does he instruct Timothy in this way?

_____

_____

_____

_____

4) What new insights about the glory of God do you gain from Paul's glorious description (vv. 14–16)?

_____

_____

_____

GOING DEEPER

Paul reminds us that our God is majestic and awesome. God is the Source of all that we could ever need in life, therefore when we pursue God and His glory, we will experience true contentment. The Old Testament prophet, Isaiah, also experienced the glory of God. Read Isaiah 6:1–8.

1   *In the year that King Uzziah died, I saw the Lord sitting on a throne, high and lifted up, and the train of His robe filled the temple.*

2   *Above it stood seraphim; each one had six wings: with two he covered his face, with two he covered his feet, and with two he flew.*

3   *And one cried to another and said: "Holy, holy, holy is the LORD of hosts; the whole earth is full of His glory!"*

4   *And the posts of the door were shaken by the voice of him who cried out, and the house was filled with smoke.*

5   *So I said: "Woe is me, for I am undone! Because I am a man of unclean lips, and I dwell in the midst of a people of unclean lips; for my eyes have seen the King, the LORD of hosts."*

6   *Then one of the seraphim flew to me, having in his hand a live coal which he had taken with the tongs from the altar.*

7   *And he touched my mouth with it, and said: "Behold, this has touched your lips; your iniquity is taken away, and your sin purged."*

8   *Also I heard the voice of the Lord, saying: "Whom shall I send, and who will go for Us?" Then I said, "Here am I! Send me."*

EXPLORING THE MEANING

5) What happened to Isaiah when he saw the Lord high and lifted up?

_____

_____

_____

_____

6) How is this scene reminiscent of the charge given to Timothy in verses 13–16?

_____

_____

_____

_____

7) Read Isaiah 43:13. What does this verse proclaim about the God whom Timothy is being charged to serve? How do you think this attribute of God would encourage Timothy or other men in his position?

_____

_____

_____

_____

(Verses to consider: Deut. 4:35; 1 Kings 8:23; Ps. 18:31; Isa. 45:5–6, 21–22)

8) For more insight about money matters, read 2 Corinthians 9:6–7. What does this passage say should be our attitude toward money and giving?

_____

_____

_____

_____

(Verses to consider: Prov. 27:24; Eccl. 5:15; Mark 8:36; Phil. 4:11)

Truth for Today

What are the danger signs of loving money? First, those who love money are more concerned with making it than with honesty, or giving a quality effort. Believers must pursue truth and excellence, for which money may be the reward. Second, those who love money never have enough. Like the leech's daughters of Proverbs 30:15, all they can say is "Give, give." Such people stand in sharp contrast to Paul, who wrote to the Philippians, "I have learned to be content in whatever circumstances I am" (Phil. 4:11). Third, those who love money tend to flaunt it. They derive an inordinate pleasure from wearing, driving, or living in what money buys. Fourth, those who love money resent giving it. They want to use it all for their own selfish gratification. Lastly, those who love money will often sin to get it. They will cheat on their income tax or their expense account, or pilfer from work. Those who compromise their principles for money betray a heart that loves money more than God, righteousness, and truth.

Reflecting on the Text

9) In what ways are you guilty of loving money? How can you overcome this sinful tendency?

_____

_____

_____

_____

_____

_____

10) How does your view of money affect your level of contentment in life?

_____

_____

_____

_____

_____

11) How fiercely and intensely are you fighting "the good fight of faith"? What would a renewed commitment to the battle look like in your life today?

_____

_____

_____

_____

_____

12) Compose your own "doxology" to God (see Paul's example in 6:15–16). What attributes of God are most amazing to you?

_____

_____

_____

_____

_____

PERSONAL RESPONSE

Write out additional reflections, questions you may have, or a prayer.

_____

_____

_____

_____

_____

_____

_____

_____

ADDITIONAL NOTES

Introduction to 2 Timothy

This epistle is the second of two inspired letters Paul wrote to his son in the faith, Timothy. For biographical information on Timothy, see the "Introduction to 1 Timothy." It is titled with the name of the addressee (1:2), as are Paul's other personal letters to individuals (Timothy, Titus, and Philemon).

Author and Date

For discussion of Paul's authorship of the Pastoral Epistles see the "Introduction to 1 Timothy: Author and Date." Paul wrote this final epistle shortly before his martyrdom, about AD 67.

Background and Setting

Paul was released from his first Roman imprisonment for a short period of ministry, during which he wrote 1 Timothy and Titus. However, in the book of 2 Timothy we find Paul once again in a Roman prison (1:16; 2:9), apparently rearrested as part of Nero's persecution of Christians. Unlike Paul's confident hope of release during his first imprisonment (Phil. 1:19, 25–26; 2:24; Philem. 22), this time he had no such hopes (4:6–8). In his first imprisonment in Rome (about AD 60–62), before Nero had begun the persecution of Christians (AD 64), he was only under house arrest and had opportunity for much interaction with people and ministry (Acts 28:16–31). At this time, five or six years later (about AD 66–67), however, he was in a cold cell (4:13), in chains (2:9), and with no hope of deliverance (4:6). Abandoned by virtually all of those close to him for fear of persecution (see 1:15; 4:9–12, 16) and facing imminent execution, Paul wrote to Timothy, urging him to hasten to Rome for one last visit with the apostle (4:9, 21). Whether Timothy made it to Rome before Paul's execution is not known. According to tradition, Paul was not released from this second Roman imprisonment but suffered the martyrdom he had foreseen (4:6).

In this letter, Paul, aware the end was near, passed the non-apostolic mantle of ministry to Timothy (see 2:2) and exhorted him to continue faithful in his duties (1:6), hold on to sound doctrine (1:13–14), avoid error (2:15–18), accept persecution for the gospel (2:3–4; 3:10–12), put his confidence in the Scripture, and preach it relentlessly (3:15–4:5).

HISTORICAL AND THEOLOGICAL THEMES

It seems that Paul may have had reason to fear that Timothy was in danger of weakening spiritually. This would have been a grave concern for Paul since Timothy needed to carry on Paul's work (see 2:2). While there are no historical indications elsewhere in the New Testament as to why Paul was so concerned, there is evidence in the epistle itself from what he wrote. This concern is evident, for example, in Paul's exhortation to "stir up" his gift (1:6), to replace fear with power, love, and a sound mind (1:7), to not be ashamed of Paul and the Lord, but willingly suffer for the gospel (1:8), and to hold on to the truth (1:13–14). Summing up the potential problem of Timothy, who might be weakening under the pressure of the church and the persecution of the world, Paul calls him to (1) generally "be strong" (2:11), the key exhortation of the first part of the letter, and to (2) continue to "preach the word" (4:2), the main admonition of the last part. These final words to Timothy include few commendations but many admonitions, including about twenty-five imperatives.

Since Timothy was well versed in Paul's theology, the apostle did not instruct him further doctrinally. He did, however, allude to several important doctrines, including salvation by God's sovereign grace (1:9–10; 2:10), the Person of Christ (2:8; 4:1, 8), and perseverance (2:11–13); plus Paul wrote the crucial text of the New Testament on the inspiration of Scripture (3:16–17).

INTERPRETIVE CHALLENGES

This letter contains no major challenges involving theological issues. There is limited data regarding several individuals named in the epistle; for example, Phygellus and Hermogenes (1:15), Onesiphorus (1:17; see 4:19), Hymenaeus and Philetus (2:17–18), Jannes and Jambres (3:8), and Alexander (4:14).

8

NOT ASHAMED

DRAWING NEAR

In this second epistle Paul knew his time left on earth was short, so he tries to motivate Timothy to persevere in the faith. What motivates you to keep growing spiritually? Why?

_____

_____

_____

Have you ever felt ashamed of being a Christian? If so, what attitudes or fears keep you from holding fast to the faith?

_____

_____

_____

THE CONTEXT

The first five verses of this letter comprise a beautiful greeting from the apostle Paul to his young protégé, serving as a pastor in Ephesus. Scholars agree this is the last letter ever penned by Paul. This motivating salutation is relevant not only to a first-century Christian leader but also to modern-day Christians—parents, Sunday-school teachers, church staff members, missionaries, students, neighbors, and friends. In short, it contains wise principles for any and every believer who wants to grow in his or her faith and who desires to be used by God to make a difference in the lives of others. It portrays a beautiful example of servanthood and love.

Paul focuses on the issue of "not being ashamed of Christ." Paul bases his appeal on the motivations for serving Christ given in the first five verses. By helping Timothy remember the apostle's authority, his unselfish concern for others, his heart of gratitude, his habits of faithful intercession, his expressed affection, and his frequent words of affirmation, Paul hopes to generate within his young colleague a courageous, unapologetic witness and obedience to the will of the Lord. Only a holy boldness (like that modeled by Paul) will enable Timothy to persevere in the face of increasing hostility.

KEYS TO THE TEXT

Spiritual Gifts: The Greek word for *spiritual* literally means "pertaining to the Spirit." Spiritual gifts are divine enablements for ministry that the Holy Spirit gives in some measure to all believers. They should be exercised under the Spirit's control and used for the building of the church to Christ's glory. The word *gifts* comes from the Greek word *charisma,* and means essentially "gift of grace" or "free gift."

Holy Calling: As always in the New Testament epistles, this calling is not a general invitation to sinners to believe the gospel and be saved; rather, it refers to God's effectual call of the elect to salvation. This calling results in holiness—first our imputed holiness (known as *justification*), then our imparted holiness (known as *sanctification*), and finally our completed holiness (that is, our *glorification*).

UNLEASHING THE TEXT

Read 1:1–18, noting the key words and definitions next to the passage.

2 Timothy 1:1–18 (NKJV)

apostle of Jesus Christ by the will of God (v. 1)—An apostle was "one who is sent with a commission." An apostle was chosen and trained by Jesus Christ to proclaim His truth during the formative years of the church. Paul's call was according to God's sovereign plan and purpose (see 1 Cor. 1:1; 2 Cor. 1:1; Eph. 1:1; Col. 1:1).

promise of life . . . in Christ Jesus (v. 1)—the gospel, which promises that those who are spiritually dead, but by faith

1 Paul, an apostle of Jesus Christ by the will of God, according to the promise of life which is in Christ Jesus,

2 To Timothy, a beloved son: Grace, mercy, and peace from God the Father and Christ Jesus our Lord.

3 I thank God, whom I serve with a pure conscience, as my forefathers did, as without ceasing I remember you in my prayers night and day,

4 greatly desiring to see you, being mindful of your tears, that I may be filled with joy,

embrace the gospel's message, will be united to Christ and find eternal life in Him (John 3:16; 10:10; 14:6; Col. 3:4).

Timothy, a beloved son (v. 2)—Only Timothy and Titus received this special expression of Paul's favor. The Greek word for "son" is better translated "child," which emphasizes Paul's role as spiritual father to Timothy.

Grace . . . our Lord (v. 2)—More than a standard greeting by Paul, this expressed his genuine desire for God's best in Timothy's life.

greatly desiring to see you (v. 4)—Because of Paul's affection for Timothy and the urgency of the hour in Paul's life, as he faced death, Paul had an intense yearning to see Timothy again (see 4:9, 13, 21).

mindful of your tears (v. 4)—Paul perhaps remembered this occurring at their latest parting, which occurred after a short visit to Ephesus, following the writing of 1 Timothy, and prior to Paul's arrest at Troas (see note on 4:13) and his second imprisonment in Rome. Years before, Paul had a similar parting with the elders at Ephesus.

5 when I call to remembrance the genuine faith that is in you, which dwelt first in your grandmother Lois and your mother Eunice, and I am persuaded is in you also.

6 Therefore I remind you to stir up the gift of God which is in you through the laying on of my hands.

7 For God has not given us a spirit of fear, but of power and of love and of a sound mind.

8 Therefore do not be ashamed of the testimony of our Lord, nor of me His prisoner, but share with me in the sufferings for the gospel according to the power of God,

9 who has saved us and called us with a holy calling, not according to our works, but according to His

Lois . . . Eunice (v. 5)—Mention of their names suggests that Paul knew them personally, perhaps because he (with Barnabas) led them to faith in Christ during his first missionary journey (see Acts 13:13–14:21). The women were true Old Testament Jewish believers, who understood the Scripture well enough to prepare themselves and Timothy (3:15) to immediately accept Jesus as Messiah when they first heard the gospel from Paul.

stir up the gift of God (v. 6)—This seems to indicate Paul was unsatisfied with Timothy's level of current faithfulness. "Stir up" means literally "to keep the fire alive," and "gift" refers to the believer's spiritual gift (regarding Timothy's spiritual gift, see notes on 4:2–6; 1 Tim. 4:14). Paul reminds Timothy that as a steward of his God-given gift for preaching, teaching, and evangelizing, he could not let it fall into disuse.

laying on of my hands (v. 6)—See 1 Timothy 4:14; 5:22; 6:12. Paul might have done this at the time of Timothy's conversion, in which case it would have corresponded to when Timothy received his spiritual gift. The expression may also refer to an extraordinary spiritual endowment, which was received or enhanced at some point after his conversion.

a spirit of fear (v. 7)—The Greek word, which can also be translated "timidity," denotes a cowardly, shameful fear caused by a weak, selfish character. The threat of Roman persecution, which was escalating under Nero, the hostility of those in the Ephesian church who resented Timothy's leadership, and the assaults of false teachers with their sophisticated systems of deceptions may have been overwhelming Timothy. But if he was fearful, it didn't come from God.

power (v. 7)—Positively, God has already given believers all the spiritual resources they need for every trial and threat (see Matt. 10:19–20). Divine power—effective, productive spiritual energy—belongs to believers (Eph. 1:18–20; 3:20; see also Zech. 4:6).

love (v. 7)—See the note on 1 Timothy 1:5. This kind of love centers on pleasing God and seeking others' welfare before one's own (see Rom. 14:8; Gal. 5:22, 25; Eph. 3:19; 1 Pet. 1:22; 1 John 4:18).

sound mind (v. 7)—This refers to a disciplined, self-controlled, and properly prioritized mind. This is the opposite of fear and cowardice that causes disorder and confusion. Focusing on the sovereign nature and perfect purposes of our eternal God allows believers to control their lives with godly wisdom and confidence in every situation (see Rom. 12:3; 1 Tim. 3:2; Titus 1:8; 2:2).

the testimony of our Lord (v. 8)—This refers to the gospel message concerning Jesus Christ. Paul did not want Timothy to be "ashamed" to name the name of Christ because he was afraid of the potential persecution (see vv. 12, 16).

me His prisoner (v. 8)—Being linked to Paul, who was a prisoner because of his preaching of the gospel, could have put Timothy's life and freedom in jeopardy (see Heb. 13:23).

not . . . works, but . . . grace (v. 9)—This truth is the foundation of the gospel. Salvation is by grace through faith, apart from works (see Rom. 3:20–25; Gal. 3:10, 11; Eph. 2:8–9; Phil. 3:8–9). Grace is also the basis for God's sustaining work in believers (see Phil. 1:6; Jude 24–25).

according to His own purpose (v. 9)—God's sovereign plan of election

in Christ Jesus (v. 9)—His sacrifice made God's salvation plan possible, because He became the substitute sacrifice for the sins of God's people (see 2 Cor. 5:21).

before time began (v. 9)—The same Greek phrase appears in Titus 1:2. The destiny of God's chosen was determined and sealed from eternity past (John 17:24; see Eph. 1:4–5; Phil. 1:29; 1 Pet. 1:2).

appearing (v. 10)—"Epiphany" is the English equivalent of this Greek word, which is most often used of Christ's second coming (4:18; 1 Tim. 6:14; Titus 2:13), but here of His first coming.

own purpose and grace which was given to us in Christ Jesus before time began,

10 but has now been revealed by the appearing of our Savior Jesus Christ, who has abolished death and brought life and immortality to light through the gospel,

11 to which I was appointed a preacher, an apostle, and a teacher of the Gentiles.

12 For this reason I also suffer these things; nevertheless I am not ashamed, for I know whom I have believed and am persuaded that He is able to keep what I have committed to Him until that Day.

13 Hold fast the pattern of sound words which you have heard from me, in faith and love which are in Christ Jesus.

14 That good thing which was committed to you, keep by the Holy Spirit who dwells in us.

abolished death . . . immortality to light (v. 10)—"Abolished" means "rendered inoperative." Physical death still exists, but it is no longer a threat or an enemy for Christians (1 Cor. 15:54–55; Heb. 2:14). It was not until the Incarnation and the gospel that God chose to fully make known the truth of immortality and eternal life, a reality only partially understood by Old Testament believers (see Job 19:26).

preacher . . . teacher (v. 11)—See 1 Timothy 2:7.

I also suffer (v. 12)—See verse 8; see also 2 Corinthians 4:8–18; 6:4–10; 11:23–28; Galatians 6:17; Philippians 3:10.

I am not ashamed (v. 12)—Paul had no fear of persecution and death from preaching the gospel in a hostile setting, because he was so confident God had sealed his future glory and blessing (see Rom. 1:16).

know whom I have believed (v. 12)—"Know" describes the certainty of Paul's intimate, saving knowledge—the object of which was God Himself. The form of the Greek verb translated "I have believed" refers to something that began in the past and has continuing results. This knowing is equal to "the knowledge of the truth" (3:7; 1 Tim. 2:4).

He is able to keep (v. 12)—See Jude 24–25.

what I have committed (v. 12)—Paul's life in time and eternity had been given to his Lord. He lived with unwavering confidence and boldness because of the revealed truth about God's power and faithfulness, and his own experience of an unbreakable relationship to the Lord (Rom. 8:31–39).

that Day (v. 12)—This is also called "Day of Christ" (see Phil. 1:10), when believers will stand before the judgment seat and be rewarded (see 1 Cor. 3:13; 2 Cor. 5:10; 1 Pet. 1:5).

sound words (v. 13)—See 1 Timothy 4:6; 6:3. This refers to the Scripture and the doctrine it teaches.

from me (v. 13)—Paul had been the source of this divine revelation (see 2:2; 3:10, 14; Phil. 4:9).

faith and love . . . in Christ Jesus (v. 13)—"Faith" is confidence that God's Word is true, and "love" is kindness and compassion in teaching that truth (see Eph. 4:15).

That good thing . . . committed to you (v. 14)—the treasure of the good news of salvation revealed in the Scripture

15 *This you know, that all those in Asia have turned away from me, among whom are Phygellus and Hermogenes.*

16 *The Lord grant mercy to the household of Onesiphorus, for he often refreshed me, and was not ashamed of my chain;*

17 *but when he arrived in Rome, he sought me out very zealously and found me.*

18 *The Lord grant to him that he may find mercy from the Lord in that Day—and you know very well how many ways he ministered to me at Ephesus.*

Asia (v. 15)—a Roman province that is part of modern Turkey; this is not a reference to the entire region of Asia Minor

Phygellus and Hermogenes (v. 15)—Nothing else is known about these two men, who apparently had shown promise as leaders, had been close to Paul, and were well known among the Asian churches, but deserted Paul under the pressure of persecution.

Onesiphorus (v. 16)—This was one of Paul's loyal coworkers who had not deserted Paul but had befriended him in prison and was not ashamed or afraid to visit the apostle there regularly and minister to his needs. Since Paul asks Timothy to greet those in his house (4:19), the family obviously lived in or near Ephesus.

when he arrived in Rome (v. 17)—Onesiphorus was perhaps on a business trip and the text implies that his search involved time, effort, and possibly even danger.

Ephesus (v. 18)—Onesiphorus's faithfulness began here many years earlier, when Paul ministered on his third or fourth missionary journey.

1) How does Paul attempt to motivate his "beloved son" in the faith?

_____

_____

_____

2) Paul offered a number of ways that Timothy could resist being ashamed of the gospel (vv. 6–14). Summarize these.

_____

_____

_____

3) Why did Paul share with Timothy the contrasting actions of his associates in ministry (1:15–18)? How was he hoping to both challenge and encourage Timothy through this?

_____

_____

_____

GOING DEEPER

In Paul and Timothy's day, suffering for their faith was common. Read about another apostle's experience of persecution in Acts 4:1–21.

1 Now as they spoke to the people, the priests, the captain of the temple, and the Sadducees came upon them,

2 being greatly disturbed that they taught the people and preached in Jesus the resurrection from the dead.

3 And they laid hands on them, and put them in custody until the next day, for it was already evening.

4 However, many of those who heard the word believed; and the number of the men came to be about five thousand.

5 And it came to pass, on the next day, that their rulers, elders, and scribes,

6 as well as Annas the high priest, Caiaphas, John, and Alexander, and as many as were of the family of the high priest, were gathered together at Jerusalem.

7 And when they had set them in the midst, they asked, "By what power or by what name have you done this?"

8 Then Peter, filled with the Holy Spirit, said to them, "Rulers of the people and elders of Israel:

9 If we this day are judged for a good deed done to a helpless man, by what means he has been made well,

10 let it be known to you all, and to all the people of Israel, that by the name of Jesus Christ of Nazareth, whom you crucified, whom God raised from the dead, by Him this man stands here before you whole.

11 This is the 'stone which was rejected by you builders, which has become the chief cornerstone.'

12 Nor is there salvation in any other, for there is no other name under heaven given among men by which we must be saved."

13 Now when they saw the boldness of Peter and John, and perceived that they were uneducated and untrained men, they marveled. And they realized that they had been with Jesus.

14 And seeing the man who had been healed standing with them, they could say nothing against it.

15 But when they had commanded them to go aside out of the council, they conferred among themselves,

16 saying, "What shall we do to these men? For, indeed, that a notable miracle has been done through them is evident to all who dwell in Jerusalem, and we cannot deny it.

17 *But so that it spreads no further among the people, let us severely threaten them, that from now on they speak to no man in this name."*

18 *So they called them and commanded them not to speak at all nor teach in the name of Jesus.*

19 *But Peter and John answered and said to them, "Whether it is right in the sight of God to listen to you more than to God, you judge.*

20 *For we cannot but speak the things which we have seen and heard."*

21 *So when they had further threatened them, they let them go, finding no way of punishing them, because of the people, since they all glorified God for what had been done.*

EXPLORING THE MEANING

4) What impresses you about the apostles' demeanor in this passage?

_____

_____

_____

_____

_____

5) Why do you think they could be so bold?

_____

_____

_____

_____

6) Read Psalm 119:46. What attitude does the psalmist demonstrate in this verse? Why is this an important attitude for believers to have?

_____

_____

_____

_____

_____

7) Read 1 Peter 4:10–11. How does God want us to use our gifts? To what end?

_____

_____

_____

_____

(Verses to consider: Rom. 12:3–7; Eph. 4:11–16; 1 Tim. 4:14)

TRUTH FOR TODAY

Faithful ministry in the Lord's service is always bittersweet. It brings suffering and joy, disappointment and gratitude. Duty can bring the deepest pain or the highest joy. Spiritual duty unfulfilled brings untold dissatisfaction, regret, and anguish, no matter how easy unfaithfulness may be. On the other hand, spiritual duty fulfilled brings untold satisfaction and happiness, whatever the cost of faithfulness. The Christian who is obedient to his duty under the Lord can say with Peter, "If anyone suffers as a Christian, let him not feel ashamed, but in that name let him glorify God" (1 Pet. 4:16).

REFLECTING ON THE TEXT

8) Have you ever suffered or been made fun of because of your faith in Jesus? Explain what happened.

_____

_____

_____

_____

9) What are your spiritual gifts (or gift)? (If you don't know, what steps can you take to discover them?)

_____

_____

_____

_____

10) What would it look like in your life to "stir up" your gift? How would this benefit the church of which you are a member?

_____

_____

_____

_____

_____

11) If God has indeed given you a spirit of power (1:7) and not of fear, in what ways can you hold fast to the truth of the gospel? What ministry or outreach can you attempt for God's glory this week?

_____

_____

_____

_____

_____

12) Perhaps you know a younger believer like Timothy. Name two things you could do to encourage this young saint to have a bolder Christian walk.

_____

_____

_____

_____

_____

Personal Response

Write out additional reflections, questions you may have, or a prayer.

_____

_____

_____

_____

_____

_____

_____

_____

_____

_____

_____

_____

_____

_____

_____

_____

_____

_____

_____

_____

_____

_____

_____

_____

9

BE DILIGENT

DRAWING NEAR

Think about any experiences you have had (or have heard about) in the following spheres:

⌒ serving in the military

⌒ playing an organized sport

⌒ farming (or having a garden)

_____

_____

_____

_____

Describe one difficult aspect of this activity.

_____

_____

_____

Describe one life lesson you learned through doing it.

_____

_____

_____

THE CONTEXT

The apostle Paul wrote to Timothy, pastor at Ephesus, because he sensed the young man was vacillating. Perhaps he was questioning his gifts, his calling, or his likely success. Facing obvious difficulties, whatever their nature, Timothy was clearly discouraged. The gist of Paul's counsel was that Timothy did not need more from God; rather, he needed to appropriate all that God had already given him. He needed encouragement to be diligent, to use his gifts, and to resist the false teachers that had infiltrated the flock.

Paul discussed several important elements of a strong and vibrant Christian life and used the vivid pictures of a teacher, a soldier, an athlete, and a farmer. Perhaps anticipating questions from Timothy, Paul then offered some powerful motives for faithfulness. From there Paul moved to inspire and encourage Timothy to be, first and foremost, a man of the Word. He urged the young pastor to maintain a firm hold on the truth and to pass that truth on to others. Only a thorough knowledge of the Scriptures would enable Timothy to recognize, resist, and rebuke falsehood. If Timothy wanted to be acceptable to God and prepared for every good work, he would have to avoid sin and walk in purity. No matter where you are in your Christian walk, you will find practical, convicting, and encouraging counsel.

KEYS TO THE TEXT

Diligence: This word denotes zealous persistence in accomplishing a goal. Timothy, like all who preach or teach the Word, was to give his maximum effort to impart God's Word completely, accurately, and clearly to his hearers.

Word of Truth: This refers to all of Scripture in general and the gospel message in particular (John 17:17; Eph. 1:13; Col. 1:5). God's Word is sufficient, comprehensive, completely without error, and able to meet every need and fulfill the desires of every heart. If we obey it, we will be blessed in whatever we do. Spiritual leaders must once again embrace the sufficiency of Scripture and call their people back to it. Individual Christians must covenant with God to be men and women of the Word, finding their resources there and applying them to every aspect of their lives. You'll never know what the Word can do if you don't study and apply it. It isn't enough to simply say you believe it. It must occupy an exalted place in your life. Since God Himself exalts it and magnifies it (Ps. 138:2), we should do likewise.

UNLEASHING THE TEXT

Read 2:1–26, noting the key words and definitions next to the passage.

2 Timothy 2:1–26 (NKJV)

my son (v. 1)—Paul had led Timothy to Christ during his first missionary journey (see 1 Cor. 4:17; 1 Tim. 1:2, 18).

1 *You therefore, my son, be strong in the grace that is in Christ Jesus.*

be strong (v. 1)—Here is the main admonition in the first part of the letter. Paul is calling for Timothy to overcome his apparent drift toward weakness and renew his commitment to his ministry.

2 *And the things that you have heard from me among many witnesses, commit these to faithful men who will be able to teach others also.*

3 *You therefore must endure hardship as a good soldier of Jesus Christ.*

4 *No one engaged in warfare entangles himself with the affairs of this life, that he may please him who enlisted him as a soldier.*

5 *And also if anyone competes in athletics, he is not crowned unless he competes according to the rules.*

6 *The hardworking farmer must be first to partake of the crops.*

7 *Consider what I say, and may the Lord give you understanding in all things.*

heard from me (v. 2)—See the notes on 1:13; see 3:14. During Timothy's many years of close association with Paul, he had heard divine truth, which God had revealed through the apostle.

among many witnesses (v. 2)—This refers to individuals such as Silas, Barnabas, and Luke, and many others in the churches who could attest to the divine authenticity of Paul's teaching—a needed reminder to Timothy in light of the many defections at Ephesus (see 1:15).

faithful men who will be able to teach others (v. 2)—Timothy was to take the divine revelation he had learned from Paul and teach it to other faithful believers —those with proven spiritual character and giftedness, who would in turn pass on those truths to another generation. From Paul to Timothy to faithful teachers to others encompasses four generations of godly leaders. That process of spiritual reproduction, which began in the early church, is to continue until the Lord returns.

a good soldier (v. 3)—The metaphor of the Christian life as warfare (against the evil world system, the believer's sinful human nature, and Satan) is a familiar one in the New Testament (see 2 Cor. 10:3–5; Eph. 6:10–20; 1 Thess. 4:8; 1 Tim. 1:18; 4:7; 6:12). Here Paul is dealing with conflict against the hostile world and persecution (see v. 9; 1:8; 3:11–12; 4:7).

entangles himself (v. 4)—Just as a soldier called to duty is completely severed from the normal affairs of civilian life, so also must the good soldier of Jesus Christ refuse to allow the things of the world to distract him (see James 4:4; 1 John 2:15–17).

competes in athletics (v. 5)—The Greek verb expresses the effort and determination needed to compete successfully in an athletic event (see 1 Cor. 9:24). To those familiar with the Olympic Games and the Isthmian Games (held in Corinth), this would be a useful picture of spiritual effort and untiring pursuit of the victory.

crowned . . . rules (v. 5)—All an athlete's hard work and discipline will be wasted if he or she fails to compete according to the rules. This is a call to obey the Word of God in the pursuit of spiritual victory.

The hardworking farmer (v. 6)—"Hardworking" is from a Greek verb meaning "to labor to the point of exhaustion." Ancient farmers worked long hours of backbreaking labor under all kinds of conditions, with the hope that their physical effort would be rewarded by a good harvest. Paul is urging Timothy not to be lazy or indolent, but to labor intensely (see Col. 1:28–29) with a view to the harvest (see 1 Cor. 3:6–7).

Consider (v. 7)—The Greek word denotes clear perception, full understanding, and careful consideration. The form of the verb suggests a strong admonition by Paul, not mere advice, to give deep thought to what he was writing.

Remember . . . Jesus Christ (v. 8)—The supreme model of a faithful teacher (v. 2), soldier (vv. 3–4), athlete (v. 5), and farmer (v. 6). Timothy was to follow His example in teaching, suffering, pursuing the prize, and planting the seeds of truth for a spiritual harvest.

of the seed of David (v. 8)—As David's descendant, Jesus is the rightful heir to his throne (Luke 1:32–33). The Lord's humanity is stressed.

raised from the dead (v. 8)—The resurrection of Christ is the central truth of the Christian faith (1 Cor. 15:3–4, 17, 19). By it, God affirmed the perfect redemptive work of Jesus Christ (see Rom. 1:4).

8 *Remember that Jesus Christ, of the seed of David, was raised from the dead according to my gospel,*

9 *for which I suffer trouble as an evildoer, even to the point of chains; but the word of God is not chained.*

10 *Therefore I endure all things for the sake of the elect, that they also may obtain the salvation which is in Christ Jesus with eternal glory.*

11 *This is a faithful saying: For if we died with Him, we shall also live with Him.*

12 *If we endure, we shall also reign with Him. If we deny Him, He also will deny us.*

13 *If we are faithless, He remains faithful; He cannot deny Himself.*

I suffer . . . but the word . . . is not chained (v. 9)—Paul contrasts his imprisonment for the sake of the gospel to the unfettered power of the Word of God.

for the sake of the elect (v. 10)—those of the elect, having been chosen for salvation from before the world began, who had not yet come to faith in Jesus Christ (see Acts 18:10; Titus 1:1)

the salvation which is in Christ Jesus (v. 10)—There is salvation in no one else (Acts 4:12; Rom. 8:29; Eph. 1:4–5). The gospel must be proclaimed (Matt. 28:19; Acts 1:8) because the elect are not saved apart from faith in Christ (Rom. 10:14).

eternal glory (v. 10)—the ultimate outcome of salvation (see Rom. 5:2; 8:17)

faithful saying (v. 11)—The saying is in verses 11–13.

died with Him . . . live with Him (v. 11)—This refers to believers' spiritual participation in Christ's death and resurrection (Rom. 6:4–8), including also the possibility of suffering martyrdom for the sake of Christ, as the context would indicate.

endure (v. 12)—Believers who persevere give evidence of the genuineness of their faith (see Matt. 10:22; John 8:31; Rom. 2:7; Col. 1:23).

reign with Him (v. 12)—in His future eternal kingdom (Rev. 1:6; 5:10; 20:4, 6)

If we deny Him, He also will deny us (v. 12)—Speaks of a final, permanent denial, such as that of an apostate (see note on 1 Tim. 1:19), not the temporary failure of a true believer like Peter (Matt. 26:69–75). Those who so deny Christ give evidence that they never truly belonged to Him (1 John 2:19) and face the fearful reality of one day being denied by Him (Matt. 10:33).

faithless (v. 13)—This refers to a lack of saving faith, not to weak or struggling faith. Unbelievers will ultimately deny Christ because their faith was not genuine (see James 2:14–26).

He remains faithful; He cannot deny Himself. (v. 13)—As faithful as Jesus is to save those who believe in Him (John 3:16), He is equally faithful to judge those who do not (John 3:18). To act any other way would be inconsistent with His holy, unchangeable nature (see Heb. 10:23).

14 *Remind them of these things, charging them before the Lord not to strive about words to no profit, to the ruin of the hearers.*

15 *Be diligent to present yourself approved to God, a worker who does not need to be ashamed, rightly dividing the word of truth.*

16 *But shun profane and idle babblings, for they will increase to more ungodliness.*

17 *And their message will spread like cancer. Hymenaeus and Philetus are of this sort,*

18 *who have strayed concerning the truth, saying that the resurrection is already past; and they overthrow the faith of some.*

19 *Nevertheless the solid foundation of God stands, having this seal: "The Lord knows those who are His," and, "Let everyone who names the name of Christ depart from iniquity."*

strive about words (v. 14)—Arguing with false teachers, i.e., deceivers who use human reason to subvert God's Word, is not only foolish (Prov. 14:7) and futile (Matt. 7:6), but dangerous (vv. 16–17). This is the first of three warnings to avoid useless arguments (see 1 Tim. 4:6–7; 6:3–5; 2 Pet. 1–3).

ruin (v. 14)—The Greek word means "overturned," or "overthrown." It appears only one other time in the New Testament (2 Pet. 2:6), where it describes the destruction of Sodom and Gomorrah. Because it replaces the truth with lies, false teaching brings spiritual catastrophe to those who heed it. The ruin can be eternal.

rightly dividing (v. 15)—Literally "cutting it straight," this refers to the exactness demanded by such trades as carpentry, masonry, and Paul's trade of leatherworking and tentmaking. Precision and accuracy are required in biblical interpretation beyond all other enterprises because the interpreter is handling God's Word. Anything less is shameful.

shun profane and idle babblings (v. 16)—Such destructive heresy leads only to "more ungodliness." Heresy can't save or sanctify. This is Paul's second such warning (see vv. 14, 23).

cancer (v. 17)—The word refers to a disease which spreads rapidly in a deadly manner. The metaphor emphasizes the insidious danger of false teaching. It attacks and consumes one's life.

Hymenaeus (v. 17)—See the note on 1 Timothy 1:20.

Philetus (v. 17)—Alexander's replacement as Hymenaeus's accomplice

the resurrection is already past (v. 18)—Like the false teachers who troubled the Corinthians (1 Cor. 15:12), Hymenaeus and Philetus denied the reality of believers' bodily resurrection. They probably taught that believers' spiritual identification with Christ's death and resurrection (Rom. 6:4–5, 8) was the only resurrection they would experience, and that had already happened. Such heretical teaching reflects the contemporary Greek philosophical view that matter was evil and spirit was good.

overthrow the faith (v. 18)—This speaks of those whose faith was not genuine (see Matt. 24:24). Genuine saving faith cannot be finally and completely overthrown. False, non-saving faith is common (see Matt. 7:21–27; 13:18–22; John 2:23–25; 6:64–66; 8:31; 1 John 2:19).

the solid foundation of God (v. 19)—This is likely a reference to the church (see 1 Tim. 3:15), which cannot be overcome by the forces of hell (Matt. 16:18) and is made up of those who belong to Him.

seal (v. 19)—This is a symbol of ownership and authenticity. Paul gives two characteristics of those with the divine seal of authenticity.

"The Lord knows those who are His" (v. 19)—This is likely a reference to Numbers 16:5. He "knows," not in the sense of awareness, but as a husband knows his wife, in the sense of intimate relationship (see John 10:27–28; Gal. 4:9). God has known His own ever since He chose them before time began.

"Let everyone . . . depart from iniquity." (v. 19)—This statement is likely adapted from Numbers 16:26 and reflects a second mark of God's ownership of believers, their pursuit of holiness (see 1 Cor. 6:19–20; 1 Pet. 1:15–16).

vessels (v. 20)—The Greek word is very general and was used to describe various tools, utensils, and furniture found in the home. In this "great house" analogy, Paul contrasts two kinds of utensils or serving dishes.

some for honor (v. 20)—In a wealthy home, the ones made of precious "gold and silver" were used for honorable purposes such as serving food to the family and guests.

some for dishonor (v. 20)—Those made of "wood and clay" were not for any honorable use, but rather those uses which were repulsive—disposing of garbage and the filthy waste of the household (see 2 Cor. 4:7).

anyone (v. 21)—This refers to whoever wants to be useful to the Lord for noble purposes. Even a common wood bucket or clay pot becomes useful when purged and made holy.

20 But in a great house there are not only vessels of gold and silver, but also of wood and clay, some for honor and some for dishonor.

21 Therefore if anyone cleanses himself from the latter, he will be a vessel for honor, sanctified and useful for the Master, prepared for every good work.

22 Flee also youthful lusts; but pursue righteousness, faith, love, peace with those who call on the Lord out of a pure heart.

23 But avoid foolish and ignorant disputes, knowing that they generate strife.

24 And a servant of the Lord must not quarrel but be gentle to all, able to teach, patient,

25 in humility correcting those who are in opposition, if God perhaps will grant them repentance, so that they may know the truth,

26 and that they may come to their senses and escape the snare of the devil, having been taken captive by him to do his will.

cleanses himself (v. 21)—The Greek word means "to thoroughly clean out," or "to completely purge." For any wastebucket in the house to be used for a noble purpose, it would have had to be vigorously scoured, cleansed, and purged of all vestiges of its former filth.

the latter (v. 21)—This refers to the vessels of dishonor (v. 20). Associating with anyone who teaches error and lives in sin is corrupting (Prov. 1:10–19; 13:20; 1 Cor. 5:6, 11; 15:33; Titus 1:16)—all the more so when they are leaders in the church. This is clearly a call to separate from all who claim to serve God, but do so as filthy implements useful only for the most dishonorable duties.

youthful lusts (v. 22)—not merely illicit sexual desires, but also such lusts as pride, desire for wealth and power, jealousy, self-assertiveness, and an argumentative spirit

disputes . . . strife (v. 23)—Paul's third warning to avoid useless arguments with false teachers (see notes on vv. 14, 16)

able to teach (v. 24)—This is one word in Greek meaning "skilled in teaching" (see note on 1 Tim. 3:2).

those who are in opposition (v. 25)—This refers primarily to unbelievers (captive to Satan, v. 26), but also could include believers deceived by the "foolish and ignorant" (v. 23) speculations of the false teachers; and, possibly, the false teachers themselves.

God . . . will grant them repentance (v. 25)—All true repentance is produced by God's sovereign grace (Eph. 2:7), and without such grace human effort to change is futile.

know the truth (v. 25)—See the note on 3:7. When God, by grace, grants saving faith, it includes the granting of repentance from sin. Neither is a human work.

the snare of the devil (v. 26)—Deception is Satan's trap. He is an inveterate, scheming, clever, and subtle purveyor of lies (see Gen. 3:4–6; John 8:44; 2 Cor. 11:13–15; Rev. 12:9).

1) Paul uses three analogies to highlight several indispensable qualities of a strong spiritual life (2:1–7). What is the main point of each analogy?

_____

_____

_____

_____

2) Summarize the beliefs and convictions that enabled Paul to persevere in a life of sacrificial ministry (vv. 8–13).

_____

_____

_____

_____

3) What kind of false teaching did Timothy combat in the Ephesian church (vv. 14–19)? What antidote does Paul offer Timothy for this teaching?

_____

_____

_____

_____

(Verses to consider: Matt. 24:24; 1 Thess. 2:4; 1 Tim. 1:3–4, 18–19; 2 Pet. 2:1–2)

4) Note the illustration of a house containing vessels for honor and for dishonor (2:20–26). How do the two differ? How does an individual go from being a vessel for dishonor to a vessel for honor?

_____

_____

_____

_____

Going Deeper

For more encouragement to stay faithful, read Romans 8:31–39.

31 *What then shall we say to these things? If God is for us, who can be against us?*

32 *He who did not spare His own Son, but delivered Him up for us all, how shall He not with Him also freely give us all things?*

33 *Who shall bring a charge against God's elect? It is God who justifies.*

34 *Who is he who condemns? It is Christ who died, and furthermore is also risen, who is even at the right hand of God, who also makes intercession for us.*

35 *Who shall separate us from the love of Christ? Shall tribulation, or distress, or persecution, or famine, or nakedness, or peril, or sword?*

36 *As it is written: "For Your sake we are killed all day long; We are accounted as sheep for the slaughter."*

37 *Yet in all these things we are more than conquerors through Him who loved us.*

38 *For I am persuaded that neither death nor life, nor angels nor principalities nor powers, nor things present nor things to come,*

39 *nor height nor depth, nor any other created thing, shall be able to separate us from the love of God which is in Christ Jesus our Lord.*

Exploring the Meaning

5) How does the truth conveyed in this beloved passage help you to endure through tough times?

_____

_____

_____

_____

6) Are you persuaded of God's love for you? Why or why not? How can the truths of this passage encourage you in this area?

_____

_____

_____

_____

7) Read 1 Thessalonians 2:7. How and why are gentleness and humility important traits for all Christians, but especially for Christian leaders?

_____

_____

_____

_____

_____

(Verses to consider: Prov. 15:1; 22:4; Matt. 11:29; 21:5; Gal. 5:22–23; Eph. 4:2; Phil. 2:3)

TRUTH FOR TODAY

Several years ago, engineers in New Jersey were building a bridge over the mouth of a river on the Atlantic coast. As they were putting down pilings, they came across the hull of an old ship that was buried in the sand. To keep the bridge on the planned route, the hull would have to be removed. After they tried every mechanical means they could think of, the ship remained in place. A young engineer suggested placing several large barges above the hull on either side, running cables underneath the hull, and attaching them tightly to the barges at low tide. When the tide rose, the hull was loosened some. At the next low tide the cables were tightened again, and at high tide the ship was loosened some more. After following that procedure for several cycles of tides, the ship eventually was freed. What humanly devised mechanical force could not accomplish, the immeasurably greater forces of nature accomplished easily.

Many Christians and churches are like that hull, embedded in spiritual immobility. They recognize the problem and try every human means to extricate themselves, but to no avail. But what His children cannot accomplish in their own strength, their heavenly Father can do by the power of His Spirit.

REFLECTING ON THE TEXT

8) In what areas of your spiritual life do you feel "embedded in immobility"?

_____

_____

_____

_____

_____

9) How can you exercise more diligence and discipline in your relationship with God?

_____

_____

_____

10) Paul and Timothy suffered for their faith. How do you think you might fare if you lived in a country where Christians were openly and routinely persecuted?

_____

_____

_____

11) How does knowing God's Word help you discern truth from falsehood?

_____

_____

_____

PERSONAL RESPONSE

Write out additional reflections, questions you may have, or a prayer.

_____

_____

_____

_____

_____

_____

10

EQUIPPED FOR GOOD WORKS

DRAWING NEAR

What person or persons have had the role of a spiritual mentor in your life? What significant lessons have you learned from them?

_____

_____

_____

_____

What is your favorite book of the Bible? Why?

_____

_____

_____

_____

THE CONTEXT

Paul had three great goals in life. First, he desired to know Christ intimately. Second, he was devoted to defending the truth of God (that is, the Scripture). Third, he longed to serve Christ and His church with an even greater passion than his earlier opposition to the gospel. These consuming priorities are clearly seen in this letter.

In chapter 3, Paul gives his sternest command to avoid, expose, and battle spiritual impostors and spiritual heresy in the church. By pointing out his own example of faithfulness and by reiterating their biblically based convictions, Paul urged Timothy to be a strong and faithful defender of the faith. He reminded his young colleague in ministry of the rich resource he had in the Word of God.

No other passage in the New Testament gives such a concise yet thorough description of the nature of God's Word. In a handful of verses, the power of Scripture to save sinners and sanctify believers is clearly shown. No minister and no ministry can succeed unless it is rooted in and built upon the eternal foundation of God's truth. The perils faced by Christians and the church are daunting; but they are no match for the awesome, living Word of God.

KEYS TO THE TEXT

Inspiration: The revelation of God was captured in the writings of Scripture (both Old and New Testaments) by means of "inspiration," which means "breathed out by God" or "God-breathed." Sometimes God told the Bible writers the exact words to say (e.g., Jer. 1:9), but more often He used their minds, vocabularies, and experiences to produce His own perfect infallible, inerrant Word. It is important to note that inspiration applies only to the original autographs of Scripture, not the Bible writers; there are no inspired Scripture writers, only inspired Scripture. So identified is God with His Word that when Scripture speaks, God speaks (cf. Rom. 9:17; Gal. 3:8). Scripture is called "the oracles of God" (Rom. 3:2; 1 Pet. 4:11), and cannot be altered. The Word of God was protected from human error in its original record by the ministry of the Holy Spirit. This ministry of the Spirit extended to both the part (the words) and to the whole in the original writings.

Equipped: This refers to being made fit or complete, enabled to meet all the demands of godly ministry and righteous living. Scripture is the key to this process. The Word accomplishes this in the life of the man of God and in all who follow him.

UNLEASHING THE TEXT

Read 3:1–17, noting the key words and definitions next to the passage.

2 Timothy 3:1–17 (NKJV)

the last days (v. 1)—This phrase refers to this age, the time since the first coming of the Lord Jesus.

perilous times (v. 1)—"Perilous" is used to describe the savage nature of two demon-possessed men (Matt. 8:28). The word for "times" had to do with epochs, rather than clock or calendar time. Such savage, dangerous eras or epochs will increase in frequency and severity as the return of Christ approaches (v. 13). The church age is fraught with these dangerous movements accumulating strength as the end nears.

1 But know this, that in the last days perilous times will come:

2 For men will be lovers of themselves, lovers of money, boasters, proud, blasphemers, disobedient to parents, unthankful, unholy,

3 unloving, unforgiving, slanderers, without self-control, brutal, despisers of good,

4 traitors, headstrong, haughty, lovers of pleasure rather than lovers of God,

5 having a form of godliness but denying its power. And from such people turn away!

having a form of godliness but denying its power (v. 5)—"Form" refers to outward shape or appearance. Like the unbelieving scribes and Pharisees, false teachers and their followers are concerned with mere external appearances (see Titus 1:16). Their outward form of Christianity and virtue makes them all the more dangerous.

6 *For of this sort are those who creep into households and make captives of gullible women loaded down with sins, led away by various lusts,*

7 *always learning and never able to come to the knowledge of the truth.*

8 *Now as Jannes and Jambres resisted Moses, so do these also resist the truth: men of corrupt minds, disapproved concerning the faith;*

9 *but they will progress no further, for their folly will be manifest to all, as theirs also was.*

10 *But you have carefully followed my doctrine, manner of life, purpose, faith, longsuffering, love, perseverance,*

11 *persecutions, afflictions, which happened to me at Antioch, at Iconium, at Lystra—what persecutions I endured. And out of them all the Lord delivered me.*

12 *Yes, and all who desire to live godly in Christ Jesus will suffer persecution.*

13 *But evil men and impostors will grow worse and worse, deceiving and being deceived.*

14 *But you must continue in the things which you have learned and been assured of, knowing from whom you have learned them,*

gullible women (v. 6)—Weak in virtue and the knowledge of the truth, and weighed down with emotional and spiritual guilt over their sins, these women were easy prey for the deceitful false teachers.

the knowledge of the truth (v. 7)—First Timothy 2:4 uses this same phrase, equating it with being saved. Here Paul identified those women (v. 6) and men who were often jumping from one false teacher or cult to another without ever coming to an understanding of God's saving truth in Jesus Christ. The present age, since the coming of Jesus Christ, has been loaded with perilous false teaching that can't save (see vv. 14, 16–17; 1 Tim. 4:1).

Jannes and Jambres (v. 8)—Although their names are not mentioned in the Old Testament, they were likely two of the Egyptian magicians who opposed Moses (Exod. 7:11, 22; 8:7, 18–19; 9:11). According to Jewish tradition, they pretended to become Jewish proselytes, instigated the worship of the golden calf, and were killed with the rest of the idolaters. Paul's choice of them as examples may indicate that the false teachers at Ephesus were practicing deceiving signs and wonders.

disapproved (v. 8)—The same word is translated "debased" in Romans 1:28 and comes from a Greek word meaning "useless" in the sense of being tested (like metal) and shown to be worthless.

folly . . . manifest (v. 9)—Sooner or later, it will be clear that these false teachers are lost fools, as became clear in the case of Jannes and Jambres.

persecutions (v. 11)—from a Greek verb that literally means "to put to flight." Paul had been forced to flee from Damascus (Acts 9:23–25), Pisidian Antioch (Acts 13:50), Iconium (Acts 14:6), Thessalonica (Acts 17:10), and Berea (Acts 17:14).

Antioch . . . Iconium . . . Lystra (v. 11)—As a native of Lystra (Acts 16:1), Timothy vividly recalled the persecution Paul faced in those three cities.

the Lord delivered me (v. 11)—See 4:17–18; Psalms 34:4, 6, 19; 37:40; 91:2–6, 14; Isaiah 41:10; 43:2; Daniel 3:17; Acts 26:16–17; 2 Corinthians 1:10. The Lord's repeated deliverance of Paul should have encouraged Timothy in the face of persecution by those at Ephesus who opposed the gospel.

who desire to live godly in Christ Jesus will suffer persecution (v. 12)—Faithful believers must expect persecution and suffering at the hands of the Christ-rejecting world (see John 15:18–21; Acts 14:22).

from whom you have learned (v. 14)—See the note on 1:13. To further encourage Timothy to stand firm, Paul reminds him of his godly heritage. The plural form of the pronoun "whom" suggests Timothy was indebted not just to Paul but to others as well (1:5).

from childhood (v. 15)—This is literally "from infancy." Two people whom Timothy was especially indebted to were his mother and grandmother (see note on 1:5), who faithfully taught him the truths of Old Testament Scripture from his earliest childhood, so that he was ready to receive the gospel when Paul preached it.

15 and that from childhood you have known the Holy Scriptures, which are able to make you wise for salvation through faith which is in Christ Jesus.

16 All Scripture is given by inspiration of God, and is profitable for doctrine, for reproof, for correction, for instruction in righteousness,

17 that the man of God may be complete, thoroughly equipped for every good work.

you have known the Holy Scriptures (v. 15)—literally "the sacred writings," a common designation of the Old Testament by Greek-speaking Jews

wise for salvation (v. 15)—The Old Testament Scriptures pointed to Christ (John 5:37–39) and revealed the need for faith in God's promises (Gen. 15:6; see Rom. 4:1–3). Thus, they were able to lead people to acknowledge their sin and need for justification in Christ (Gal. 3:24). Salvation is brought by the Holy Spirit using the Word.

faith which is in Christ Jesus (v. 15)—Though not understanding all the details involved (see 1 Pet. 1:10–12), Old Testament believers including Abraham (John 8:56) and Moses (Heb. 11:26) looked forward to the coming of the Messiah (Isa. 7:14; 9:6) and His atonement for sin (Isa. 53:5–6). So did Timothy, who responded when he heard the gospel.

All Scripture (v. 16)—Grammatically similar Greek constructions (Rom. 7:12; 2 Cor. 10:10; 1 Tim. 1:15; 2:3; 4:4) argue persuasively that the translation "all Scripture is given by inspiration . . ." is accurate. Both Old Testament and New Testament Scripture are included.

doctrine (v. 16)—This refers to the divine instruction or doctrinal content of both the Old Testament and the New Testament (see 2:15; Acts 20:18, 20–21, 27; 1 Cor. 2:14–16; Col. 3:16; 1 John 2:20, 24, 27). The Scripture provides the comprehensive and complete body of divine truth necessary for life and godliness (see Ps. 119:97–105).

reproof (v. 16)—This refers to rebuke for wrong behavior or wrong belief. The Scripture exposes sin (Heb. 4:12–13) that can then be dealt with through confession and repentance.

correction (v. 16)—The restoration of something to its proper condition. The word appears only here in the New Testament but was used in extrabiblical Greek of righting a fallen object or helping back to their feet those who had stumbled. Scripture not only rebukes wrong behavior but also points the way back to godly living (see Ps. 119:9–11; John 15:1–2).

instruction in righteousness (v. 16)—Scripture provides positive training ("instruction" originally referred to training a child) in godly behavior, not merely the rebuke and correction of wrong behavior (Acts 20:32; 1 Tim. 4:6; 1 Pet. 2:1–2).

man of God (v. 17)—This is a technical term for an official preacher of divine truth (see the note on 1 Tim. 6:11).

complete (v. 17)—capable of doing everything one is called to do (see Col. 2:10)

thoroughly equipped (v. 17)—Through the Scriptures, believers are enabled to meet all the demands of godly ministry and righteous living. The Word not only accomplishes this in the life of the man of God, but also in all who follow him (Eph. 4:11–13).

1) What kinds of sins did Paul say would become more prevalent in the last days (3:1–9)? Why?

_____

_____

_____

_____

_____

2) What do you learn about Paul's "mentoring" methods (3:10–14)? How did Timothy carefully follow Paul's example?

_____

_____

_____

_____

_____

3) What character qualities did Paul model for his protégé?

_____

_____

_____

_____

(Verses to consider: Acts 20:18–21; Rom. 8:18; 1 Cor. 4:16–17; Eph. 5:2; Phil. 1:17–18)

4) Look at the amazing statements about the Word of God in verses 15–17. What is its nature? Why did God give us the Scriptures?

_____

_____

_____

_____

Going Deeper

The Old Testament psalmist wrote often about the power and truth of God's Word. Read Psalm 119:9–32.

9 *How can a young man cleanse his way? By taking heed according to Your word.*

10 *With my whole heart I have sought You; oh, let me not wander from Your commandments!*

11 *Your word I have hidden in my heart, that I might not sin against You.*

12 *Blessed are You, O LORD! Teach me Your statutes.*

13 *With my lips I have declared all the judgments of Your mouth.*

14 *I have rejoiced in the way of Your testimonies, as much as in all riches.*

15 *I will meditate on Your precepts, and contemplate Your ways.*

16 *I will delight myself in Your statutes; I will not forget Your word.*

17 *Deal bountifully with Your servant, that I may live and keep Your word.*

18 *Open my eyes, that I may see wondrous things from Your law.*

19 *I am a stranger in the earth; do not hide Your commandments from me.*

20 *My soul breaks with longing for Your judgments at all times.*

21 *You rebuke the proud—the cursed, who stray from Your commandments.*

22 *Remove from me reproach and contempt, for I have kept Your testimonies.*

23 *Princes also sit and speak against me, but Your servant meditates on Your statutes.*

24 *Your testimonies also are my delight and my counselors.*

25 *My soul clings to the dust; revive me according to Your word.*

26 *I have declared my ways, and You answered me; teach me Your statutes.*

27 *Make me understand the way of Your precepts; so shall I meditate on Your wonderful works.*

28 *My soul melts from heaviness; strengthen me according to Your word.*

29 *Remove from me the way of lying, and grant me Your law graciously.*

30 *I have chosen the way of truth; Your judgments I have laid before me.*

31 *I cling to Your testimonies; O LORD, do not put me to shame!*

32 *I will run the course of Your commandments, for You shall enlarge my heart.*

EXPLORING THE MEANING

5) How would you characterize the psalmist's attitude toward God's Word?

_____

_____

_____

_____

(Verses to consider: Ps. 19; 119:69–77, 97, 103, 127–133)

6) List several benefits stated in Psalm 119 of knowing and obeying the Word.

_____

_____

_____

_____

7) Read Hebrews 4:12–13. What does this passage say about the manner in which God's Word exposes sin in a believer's life?

_____

_____

_____

_____

TRUTH FOR TODAY

The church today faces times of unparalleled difficulty and danger. As extraordinary opportunities for spreading the gospel increase with rapidity, attacks on the church are also increasing with great speed. Heresy, apostasy, self-will, and their accompanying moral decadence are engulfing the evangelical church. Like cancer cells that rebel against the body, these evils are in rebellion against God by corrupting and weakening the church, the body of Christ. Also like cancer cells, the evils multiply rapidly and choke out and destroy normal cells. Much like white cells in the blood, which will not attack cancerous cells because they are identified with the body, many naive and careless church leaders take no action against corruption in the church simply because the corruption hides behind the guise of orthodoxy. Simply put, much of the church is in rebellion against the Lord.

REFLECTING ON THE TEXT

8) Look over the list of sinful behaviors in the last days (vv. 1–7). Do you see any that you have tolerated in your own heart? If so, which ones?

_____

_____

_____

_____

9) How much does pop culture promote these very attitudes and actions? How can you respond to the cultural pull?

_____

_____

_____

_____

10) Chapter 3 makes clear that Timothy followed Paul and that Paul served as a spiritual mentor to the younger Timothy. What older and wiser Christian do you know who might be willing to serve as a mentor to you in the Christian life? Is there a younger Christian in whom you might be able to invest your life?

_____

_____

_____

11) This chapter concludes with a declaration of the inspiration and power of God's Word. How equipped by Scripture are you? Check each of the following statements that are true of your life:

_____ I have read the Bible cover to cover.

_____ I regularly take notes and listen attentively to the preached Word of God.

_____ I make it a habit to memorize Scripture.

_____ I know how to study the Bible for myself (figuring out what it says, what it means and how it applies to my life).

_____ I spend time meditating on scriptural truths that I've learned.

What needs to change in your view and approach to studying and knowing the Bible? Why is this important?

_____

_____

_____

_____

Ask God to show you how to become better equipped to serve Him, and to renew your love for His Word.

Personal Response

Write out additional reflections, questions you may have, or a prayer.

_____

_____

_____

_____

_____

_____

_____

_____

_____

ADDITIONAL NOTES

PREACHING WITH INTEGRITY

DRAWING NEAR

What is the most powerful sermon you can recall hearing? What made it so meaningful?

_____

_____

_____

_____

_____

What qualities do you identify as part of great preaching?

_____

_____

_____

_____

_____

THE CONTEXT

Paul hand-picked Timothy to pastor this growing congregation and to defend the faith, restoring the church to orthodoxy. Paul did not focus on Timothy's external success, but on his internal condition. Paul did not discuss church programs or size; on the contrary, he concentrated on church health. And since a church's health almost always mirrors the spiritual well-being of its leaders, Paul addressed Timothy's own motives and character.

In many regards, 2 Timothy is a spiritual inventory. It focuses on issues such as commitment, faithfulness, integrity, and discipline. No preacher of truth can ever be powerful in public unless and until he is first powerful in his private life. Although 4:1–5 is directed first and foremost to Timothy, it contains a valuable commission to all believers in every era. Why? Churches are obligated to hold their pastors accountable to these divine precepts.

Keys to the Text

Preaching: Preaching that does not strive to communicate God's truth to man is not legitimate preaching. The preacher who avoids doctrine because he thinks it is too technical or impractical has abdicated his biblical responsibility. Called to speak with the authority of God, the preacher must be an expositor of God's Word. Moving stories, moralistic advice, psychology, comedy, and opinion all are void of certainty. Only the authoritative proclamation of the Word fits the intent of God in the call to preach. Paul commanded Timothy to stick with the confrontational preaching of the powerful Word. There is no closed season on the Word. We must proclaim it constantly and incessantly.

Evangelist: Used only two other times in the New Testament (see Acts 21:8; Eph. 4:11), this word always refers to a specific office of ministry for the purpose of preaching the gospel to non-Christians. Based on Ephesians 4:11, it is very basic to assume that all churches would have both pastor-teachers and evangelists. But the related verb "to preach the gospel" and the related noun "gospel" are used throughout the New Testament not only in relation to evangelists but also to the call for every Christian, especially preachers and teachers, to proclaim the gospel. Paul did not call Timothy to the office of an evangelist, but to "do the work" of one.

Unleashing the Text

Read 4:1–5, noting the key words and definitions next to the passage.

2 Timothy 4:1–5 (NKJV)

I charge you (v. 1)—Or better "command"; the original Greek has the idea of issuing a forceful order or directive (see 2:14; 1 Tim. 1:18; 5:21).

1 *I charge you therefore before God and the Lord Jesus Christ, who will judge the living and the dead at His appearing and His kingdom:*

before God and the Lord Jesus Christ (v. 1)—The Greek construction also allows the translation "in the presence of God, even Christ Jesus," which is probably the best rendering since He is about to be introduced as the judge (see John 5:22). Everyone who ministers the Word of God is under the omniscient scrutiny of Christ (see 2 Cor. 2:17; Heb. 13:17).

Christ, who will judge (v. 1)—The grammatical construction suggests imminency—that Christ is about to judge. Paul is emphasizing the unique accountability that all believers, and especially ministers of the Word of God, have to Christ as Judge. Service to Christ is rendered both under His watchful eye and with the knowledge that as Judge He will one day appraise the works of every believer (see 1 Cor. 3:12–15; 4:1–5; 2 Cor. 5:10). That is not a judgment of condemnation, but one of evaluation. With regard to salvation, believers have been judged already and declared righteous—they are no longer subject to the condemnation of sin (Rom. 8:1–4).

the living and the dead (v. 1)—Christ will ultimately judge all men in three distinct settings: (1) the judgment of believers after the Rapture; (2) the sheep and goats judgment of the nations, in which

106

2 *Preach the word! Be ready in season and out of season. Convince, rebuke, exhort, with all longsuffering and teaching.*

3 *For the time will come when they will not endure sound doctrine, but according to their own desires, because they have itching ears, they will heap up for themselves teachers;*

4 *and they will turn their ears away from the truth, and be turned aside to fables.*

5 *But you be watchful in all things, endure afflictions, do the work of an evangelist, fulfill your ministry.*

believers will be separated from unbelievers (Matt. 25:31–33), for entrance into the millennial kingdom; and (3) the Great White Throne judgment of unbelievers only (Rev. 20:11–15). Here, the apostle is referring to judgment in a general sense, encompassing all those elements.

His appearing (v. 1)—The Greek word translated "appearing" literally means "a shining forth" and was used by the ancient Greeks of the supposed appearance to men of a pagan god. Here, Paul is referring generally to Christ's second coming, when He will judge "the living and the dead" (see previous note) and establish His millennial and eternal kingdom (see note on 1 Tim. 6:14).

the word (v. 2)—the entire written Word of God, His complete revealed truth as contained in the Bible (see 3:15–16; Acts 20:27)

Be ready (v. 2)—The Greek word has a broad range of meanings, including suddenness (Luke 2:9; Acts 12:7) or forcefulness (Luke 20:1; Acts 4:1; 6:12; 23:27). Here the form of the verb suggests the complementary ideas of urgency, preparedness, and readiness. It was used of a soldier prepared to go into battle or a guard who was continually alert for any surprise attack—attitudes which are imperative for a faithful preacher.

in season and out of season (v. 2)—The faithful preacher must proclaim the Word when it is popular and/or convenient, and when it is not; when it seems suitable to do so, and when it seems not. The dictates of popular culture, tradition, reputation, acceptance, or esteem in the community (or in the church) must never alter the true preacher's commitment to proclaim God's Word.

Convince, rebuke (v. 2)—This reflects the negative side of preaching the Word (the "reproof" and "correction"; see 3:16). The Greek word for "convince" refers to correcting behavior or false doctrine by using careful biblical argument to help a person understand the error of his actions. The Greek word for "rebuke" deals more with correcting the person's motives by convicting him of his sin and leading him to repentance.

exhort . . . teaching (v. 2)—the positive side of preaching (the "doctrine" and "instruction"; see 3:16)

not endure (v. 3)—This refers to holding up under adversity and can be translated "tolerate." Paul here warns Timothy that, in the dangerous seasons of this age, many people would become intolerant of the confrontational, demanding preaching of God's Word (1:13, 14; 1 Tim. 1:9–10; 6:3–5).

sound doctrine (v. 3)—See the notes on 1:13; 1 Timothy 4:6; cf. Titus 2:1.

their own desires . . . itching ears (v. 3)—Professing Christians or nominal believers in the church follow their own desires and flock to preachers who offer them God's blessings apart from His forgiveness, and His salvation apart from their repentance. They have an itch to be entertained by teachings that will produce pleasant sensations and leave them with good feelings about themselves. Their goal is that men preach "according to their own desires." Under those conditions, people will dictate what men preach, rather than God dictating it by His Word.

fables (v. 4)—This refers to false ideologies, viewpoints, and philosophies in various forms that oppose sound doctrine (see 2 Cor. 10:3–5; 1 Tim. 1:4; 4:7; Titus 1:14; 2 Pet. 1:16).

1) Why is preaching such a serious calling?

_____

_____

_____

_____

(Verses to consider: 1 Cor. 3:12–15; Gal. 1:10; James 3:1–2)

2) According to this passage, what should the job description of the preacher encompass?

_____

_____

_____

(Verses to consider: Matt. 3:1–2; 1 Cor. 2:1–5; 2 Tim. 1:13–14; 2:15; 1 Pet. 3:15)

3) What obstacles will preachers of the truth encounter in the last days?

_____

_____

_____

_____

(Verses to consider: Isa. 6:8–10; 1 Tim. 4:1–3)

GOING DEEPER

In a related passage, Paul talks further about his work. Read Colossians 1:24–29.

24 *I now rejoice in my sufferings for you, and fill up in my flesh what is lacking in the afflictions of Christ, for the sake of His body, which is the church,*

25 *of which I became a minister according to the stewardship from God which was given to me for you, to fulfill the word of God,*

26 *the mystery which has been hidden from ages and from generations, but now has been revealed to His saints.*

27 *To them God willed to make known what are the riches of the glory of this mystery among the Gentiles: which is Christ in you, the hope of glory.*

28 *Him we preach, warning every man and teaching every man in all*
wisdom, that we may present every man perfect in Christ Jesus.

29 *To this end I also labor, striving according to His working which works in*
me mightily.

EXPLORING THE MEANING

4) How does Paul describe his own preaching ministry in this passage?

_____

_____

_____

_____

_____

_____

(Verses to consider: 2 Cor. 4:5; Gal. 1:10–11)

5) What is the mystery Paul preached about?

_____

_____

_____

_____

_____

6) Read Jeremiah 5:30–31. What observation did the prophet make? How
have you seen this truth verified throughout the history of the church? How
do you see it verified currently?

_____

_____

_____

_____

_____

(Verses to consider: Ezek. 33:31–32; Acts 17:21; Rom. 1:18; 2 Cor. 4:4)

7) Read 2 Corinthians 4:4–5. How did Paul's preaching contrast with the self-centered preaching of the false teachers? What is the answer for combating false and self-centered preaching?

_____

_____

_____

_____

_____

_____

Truth for Today

There are gifted orators who can sway an audience with the power of their persuasive rhetoric. There are men who are erudite, knowledgeable, well-trained, and worldly-wise, who can cause other men to change their minds about certain matters. There are men who can relate moving stories that tug at a hearer's heart and move him emotionally. Throughout the history of the church, including our own time, God has chosen to endow some ministers with such abilities. But God also has chosen not to bless every faithful preacher in those particular ways. Nevertheless, He charges them with the same task of preaching His Word, because the spiritual power and effectiveness of preaching does not rest in the skill of the speaker, but in the truth.

Reflecting on the Text

8) How can you encourage your own preacher/pastor this week?

_____

_____

_____

_____

_____

9) Even if God hasn't called you to preach, He has called you to share His truth with others. What people in your life seem to be most receptive to the Word of God right now? What will you do to take advantage of this window of opportunity?

_____

_____

_____

_____

10) Paul used the anticipated return of Christ (and subsequent judgment) to motivate Timothy to preach faithfully. What does the second advent motivate you to change about your life?

_____

_____

_____

_____

_____

PERSONAL RESPONSE

Write out additional reflections, questions you may have, or a prayer.

_____

_____

_____

_____

_____

_____

_____

_____

_____

Additional Notes

_____

_____

_____

_____

_____

_____

_____

_____

_____

_____

_____

_____

_____

_____

_____

_____

_____

_____

_____

_____

_____

_____

_____

_____

LAST WORDS

DRAWING NEAR

Suppose you were allowed to write a short final letter to your dearest loved ones. What topics would you discuss? What counsel would you give, and why?

_____

_____

_____

Does the prospect of standing before Christ fill you with joy and anticipation, or with fear and trepidation? Why?

_____

_____

_____

THE CONTEXT

Last words are always revealing. Napoleon supposedly said, "I die before my time; and my body will be given back to the earth, to become the food of worms." Gandhi reportedly declared, "For the first time in fifty years I find myself in a slough of despond. All about me is darkness. I am praying for light." Clearly, as men and women stand on the brink of eternity, they are seldom able to mask their true feelings, thoughts, and fears.

As the apostle Paul neared the end of his life, however, he was able to look back without regret or remorse. In fact, his mood is one of triumph, and his tone is hopeful. Most scholars believe this was the last letter Paul ever wrote. In this final chapter he examines his life from three perspectives: the present reality of the end of his life, for which he was ready; the past, when he had been faithful; and the future, as he anticipated his heavenly reward.

In the closing verses of this letter, Paul brought his young ministry associate up to date on the spiritual condition, activities, and whereabouts of certain men and women who had either helped or harmed his ministry. Here we see deeply into the heart of this wonderful man of God. Read this section carefully, and you will be challenged by the examples—both good and bad—of the people who either aided or opposed Paul in his quest to live to the glory of God by helping to build up the church of Jesus Christ.

Keys to the Text

Crown of Righteousness: The Greek word for "crown" literally means "surrounding," and it was used of the plaited wreaths or garlands placed on the heads of dignitaries and victorious military officers or athletes. Linguistically, crown "of righteousness" can mean either that righteousness is the source of the crown, or that righteousness is the nature of the crown. Like the "crown of life" (James 1:12), the "crown of rejoicing" (1 Thess. 2:19), the "imperishable crown" (1 Cor. 9:25), and the "crown of glory" (1 Pet. 5:4)—in which life, rejoicing, imperishability, and glory describe the nature of the crown—the context here seems to indicate that the crown represents eternal righteousness.

Unleashing the Text

Read 4:6–22, noting the key words and definitions next to the passage.

2 Timothy 4:6–22 (NKJV)

already (v. 6)—meaning his death was imminent

a drink offering (v. 6)—in the Old Testament sacrificial system, this was the final offering that followed the burnt and grain offerings prescribed for the people of Israel (Num. 15:1–16). Paul saw his coming death as his final offering to God in a life that had already been full of sacrifices to Him.

6 For I am already being poured out as a drink offering, and the time of my departure is at hand.

7 I have fought the good fight, I have finished the race, I have kept the faith.

8 Finally, there is laid up for me the crown of righteousness, which the Lord, the righteous Judge, will give to me on that Day, and not to me only but also to all who have loved His appearing.

my departure (v. 6)—This refers to Paul's death. The Greek word essentially refers to the loosening of something, such as the mooring ropes of a ship or the ropes of a tent; thus it eventually acquired the secondary meaning of "departure."

have fought . . . have finished . . . have kept (v. 7)—The form of the three Greek verbs "have fought, have finished, have kept" indicates completed action with continuing results. Paul saw his life as complete—he had been able to accomplish through the Lord's power all that God called him to do. He was a soldier (2:3–4; 2 Cor. 10:3; 1 Tim. 6:12; Philem. 2), an athlete (1 Cor. 9:24–27; Eph. 6:12), and a guardian (1:13–14; 1 Tim. 6:20–21).

the faith (v. 7)—the truths and standards of the revealed Word of God

that Day (v. 8)—See the note on 1:12.

9 Be diligent to come to me quickly;

10 for Demas has forsaken me, having loved this present world, and has departed for Thessalonica—Crescens for Galatia, Titus for Dalmatia.

11 Only Luke is with me. Get Mark and bring him with you, for he is useful to me for ministry.

12 And Tychicus I have sent to Ephesus.

13 Bring the cloak that I left with Carpus at Troas when you come—and the books, especially the parchments.

Be diligent to come to me quickly (v. 9)—Paul longed to see his beloved co-worker, but it was imperative that Timothy make haste because Paul knew his days were numbered (v. 6).

Demas (v. 10)—He had been one of Paul's closest associates, along with Luke and Epaphras (see Col. 4:14; Philem. 24).

forsaken (v. 10)—This Greek word means "to utterly abandon," with the idea of leaving someone in a dire situation.

Demas was a fair-weather disciple who had never counted the cost of genuine commitment to Christ. His kind are described by our Lord in Matthew 13:20–21 (see John 8:31; 1 John 2:1).

loved this present world (v. 10)—See James 4:4.

Thessalonica (v. 10)—Demas may have considered this city a safe haven.

Crescens (v. 10)—In contrast to Demas, Crescens must have been faithful and dependable, since Paul sent him to Galatia, a Roman province in central Asia Minor, where Paul ministered on each of his three missionary journeys.

Titus (v. 10)—Paul's closest friend and coworker next to Timothy (Titus 1:5)

Dalmatia (v. 10)—also known as Illyricum (Rom. 15:19), a Roman province on the east coast of the Adriatic Sea, just north of Macedonia

Luke (v. 11)—the author of the Gospel of Luke and Acts, and Paul's devoted friend and personal physician, who could not carry the burden of ministry in Rome by himself

Get Mark and bring him with you (v. 11)—Evidently Mark lived somewhere along the route Timothy would take from Ephesus to Rome. The one who was the author of the Gospel of Mark (sometimes called John), cousin of Barnabas (Col. 4:10), and devoted fellow worker (Philem. 24), had once left Paul and Barnabas in shame, but had become by this time a valued servant.

Tychicus (v. 12)—Paul had either sent him to Ephesus earlier, or he was sending him there to deliver this second letter to Timothy, just as Tychicus had previously delivered Paul's letters to the churches at Ephesus (Eph. 6:12), Colosse (Col. 4:7), and possibly to Titus.

cloak (v. 13)—a large, heavy wool garment that doubled as a coat and blanket in cold weather, which Paul would soon face (v. 21)

Carpus (v. 13)—an otherwise unknown acquaintance of Paul whose name means "fruit"

Troas (v. 13)—a seaport of Phyrgia, in Asia Minor

the books, especially the parchments (v. 13)—"Books" refers to papyrus scrolls, possibly Old Testament books. "Parchments" were vellum sheets made of treated animal hides and thus extremely expensive. They may have been copies of letters he had written or blank sheets for writing other letters. That Paul did not have these already in his possession leads to the possible conclusion that he was arrested in Troas and had no opportunity to retrieve them.

Alexander the coppersmith (v. 14)—This is probably not the same man whom Paul delivered to Satan along with Hymenaeus (1 Tim. 1:20), since Paul singles him out as the one who was a "coppersmith." This Alexander, however, may have been an idol maker (see Acts 19:24).

did me much harm (v. 14)—Alexander opposed Paul's teaching and likely spread his own false doctrine. He may have been instrumental in Paul's arrest and may even have borne false witness against him (see Acts 19:23-41).

May the Lord repay him (v. 14)—Paul left vengeance in God's hands (Deut. 32:35; Rom. 12:19).

14 *Alexander the coppersmith did me much harm. May the Lord repay him according to his works.*

15 *You also must beware of him, for he has greatly resisted our words.*

16 *At my first defense no one stood with me, but all forsook me. May it not be charged against them.*

17 *But the Lord stood with me and strengthened me, so that the message might be preached fully through me, and that all the Gentiles might hear. Also I was delivered out of the mouth of the lion.*

18 *And the Lord will deliver me from every evil work and preserve me for His heavenly kingdom. To Him be glory forever and ever. Amen!*

19 *Greet Prisca and Aquila, and the household of Onesiphorus.*

first defense (v. 16)—the Greek word for "defense" gives us the English words "apology" and "apologetics." It referred to a verbal defense used in a court of law. In the Roman legal system, an accused person received two hearings: the *prima actio*, much like a contemporary arraignment, established the charge and determined if there was a need for a trial. The *secunda actio* then established the accused's guilt or innocence. The defense Paul referred to was the *prima actio*.

May it not be charged against them. (v. 16)—like Stephen (Acts 7:60) and the Lord Himself (Luke 23:24)

But the Lord stood with me (v. 17)—The Lord fulfills His promise never to "leave or forsake" His children (Deut. 31:6, 8).

the message might be preached fully through me (v. 17)—As he had done in the past (Acts 26:2-29), Paul was able to proclaim the gospel before a Roman tribunal.

all the Gentiles might hear (v. 17)—By proclaiming the gospel to such a cosmopolitan, pagan audience, Paul could say that he had reached all the Gentiles with the gospel. This was a fulfillment of his commission (Acts 9:15-16; 26:15-18).

the mouth of the lion (v. 17)—See Daniel 6:26-27. This was a common figure for mortal danger (Ps. 22:21; 35:17), which was a common occurrence for Paul (see Acts 14:19; 2 Cor. 4:8-12; 6:4-10; 11:23-27). Peter pictured Satan as a lion in 1 Peter 5:8.

will deliver me from every evil work (v. 18)—On the basis of the Lord's present work, strengthening Paul and standing with him, Paul had hope for the Lord's future work. He knew God would deliver him from all temptations and plots against him (2 Cor. 1:8-10).

preserve me for His heavenly kingdom (v. 18)—Paul knew the completion of his own salvation was nearer than when he first believed (see Rom. 13:11; 2 Cor. 5:8; Phil. 1:21).

Prisca and Aquila (v. 19)—Paul first met these two faithful friends in Corinth after they fled Italy (see note on Acts 18:2). They ministered for some time in Ephesus (Acts 18:18-19), later returned to Rome for a period of time (Rom. 16:3), and had returned to Ephesus.

the household of Onesiphorus (v. 19)—See the note on 1:16.

20 *Erastus stayed in Corinth, but Trophimus I have left in Miletus sick.*

21 *Do your utmost to come before winter. Eubulus greets you, as well as Pudens, Linus, Claudia, and all the brethren.*

22 *The Lord Jesus Christ be with your spirit. Grace be with you. Amen.*

Erastus (v. 20)—probably the city treasurer of Corinth, who sent greetings through Paul to the church at Rome (see Rom. 16:23)

Corinth (v. 20)—leading city in Greece

Trophimus (v. 20)—a native of Asia, specifically Ephesus, who had accompanied Paul from Greece to Troas (see Acts 20:4)

Miletus (v. 20)—a city and seaport in the province of Lycia, located forty miles south of Ephesus (see Acts 20:15)

before winter (v. 21)—In view of the coming season and the cold Roman jail cell, Paul needed the cloak for warmth. He would also have less opportunity to use the books and parchments as the duration of light grew shorter in winter.

Eubulus . . . Pudens, Linus, Claudia (v. 21)—The first three names are Latin, which could indicate they were from Italy and had been members in the church at Rome. "Claudia" was a believer and close friend of whom nothing else is known.

Grace be with you. (v. 22)—This is the same benediction as in Paul's previous letter to Timothy (see note on 1 Tim. 6:21). The "you" is plural, which means it extended to the entire Ephesian congregation.

1) Sensing that his time on earth was drawing to a close, how did the apostle Paul summarize his life (4:6–8)?

_____

_____

_____

_____

(Verses to consider: 2 Cor. 11:23–29; 2 Pet. 1:12–15)

2) As Paul looked to the future, what was his hope?

_____

_____

_____

_____

(Verses to consider: Prov. 24:12; Matt. 5:11–12; Phil. 3:14; Heb. 11:6)

3) Paul lists a number of individuals at the end of this epistle. What facts are revealed about each of these associates and enemies of Paul?

_____

_____

_____

_____

GOING DEEPER

After Jesus' resurrection, He appeared to His disciples. Read what Jesus commanded in Matthew 28:16–20.

16 *Then the eleven disciples went away into Galilee, to the mountain which Jesus had appointed for them.*

17 *When they saw Him, they worshiped Him; but some doubted.*

18 *And Jesus came and spoke to them, saying, "All authority has been given to Me in heaven and on earth.*

19 *Go therefore and make disciples of all the nations, baptizing them in the name of the Father and of the Son and of the Holy Spirit,*

20 *teaching them to observe all things that I have commanded you; and lo, I am with you always, even to the end of the age." Amen.*

EXPLORING THE MEANING

4) What significant truths and commands did Christ communicate in His final words? How did Paul fulfill these?

_____

_____

_____

5) What echoes of Christ's final words do you hear in Paul's last words?

_____

_____

_____

(Verses to consider: Luke 24:44–51; Acts 1:6–9)

6) Read Philippians 1:21. How did Paul view death? Why?

_____

_____

_____

_____

_____

(Verses to consider: Isa. 25:8; Hos. 13:14; 1 Cor. 9:25; 15:53–55)

TRUTH FOR TODAY

In 1904, William Borden, a member of the Borden dairy family, finished high school in Chicago and was given a world cruise as a graduation present. Particularly while traveling through the near East and Far East, he became heavily burdened for the lost. After returning home, he spent seven years at Princeton University, the first four in undergraduate work and the last three in seminary. While in school, he penned these words in the back of his Bible: "No reserves."

Although his family pleaded with him to take control of the business, which was foundering, he insisted that God's call to the mission field had priority. After disposing of his wealth, he added, "No retreat" after "No reserves." On his way to China to witness to the Muslims there, he contracted cerebral meningitis in Egypt and died within a month. After his death, someone looking through his Bible discovered these final words: "No regrets." He knew that the Lord does not require success, only faithfulness.

REFLECTING ON THE TEXT

7) How does the life of Demas serve as a warning to you today? How does the life of John Mark serve as a hopeful reminder?

_____

_____

_____

_____

_____

8) Fast forward in your mind to the end of your life. Now look back. What kind of life do you want to have lived? How do you wish to be remembered? Using the answers to those questions, make a short list of things that you want God to begin changing in your life.

---

9) What is the most meaningful lesson you've learned from your study of 1 & 2 Timothy?

---

10) How do you want your life to be different as a result?

PERSONAL RESPONSE

Write out additional reflections, questions you may have, or a prayer.

The MacArthur Bible Study Series

Revised and updated, the MacArthur Study Guide Series continues to be one of the bestselling study guide series on the market today. For small group or individual use, intriguing questions and new material take the participant deeper into God's Word.

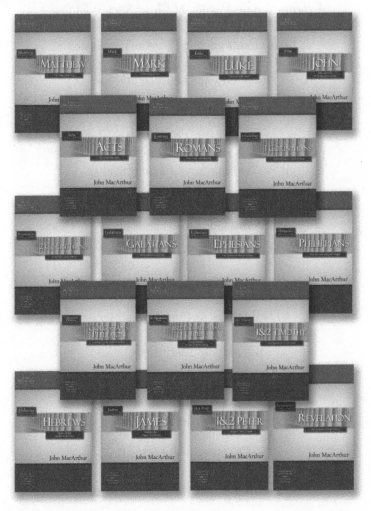

Available at your local Christian Bookstore or www.thomasnelson.com

Look for these exciting titles
by John MacArthur

Experiencing the Passion of Christ

Experiencing the Passion of Christ Student Edition

Twelve Extraordinary Women Workbook

Twelve Ordinary Men Workbook

Welcome to the Family:
What to Expect Now That You're a Christian

What the Bible Says About Parenting:
Biblical Principles for Raising Godly Children

Hard to Believe Workbook:
The High Cost and Infinite Value of Following Jesus

The John MacArthur Study Library for PDA

The MacArthur Bible Commentary

The MacArthur Study Bible, NKJV

The MacArthur Topical Bible, NKJV

The MacArthur Bible Commentary

The MacArthur Bible Handbook

The MacArthur Bible Studies series

Available at your local Christian Bookstore
or visit www.thomasnelson.com

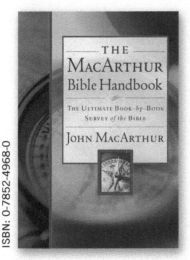
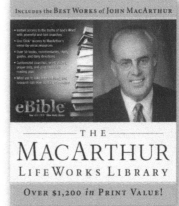